How to R___ _

Recording

Session

by
Jayce De Santis

6400 Hollis Street, Suite 12
Emeryville, CA 94608

Library of Congress Catalog Card Number: 97-71345
Book design, layout, and cover art: Linda Gough
Production staff: Mike Lawson: publisher; Lisa Duran: editor; Randy Antin: editorial assistant;
Sally Engelfried: editorial assistance; Teresa Poss: administrative assistant;
Ellen Richman: production director; Sherry Bloom: production assistant

6400 Hollis Street, Suite 12
Emeryville, CA 94608
(510) 653-3307

Also from MixBooks:

The Songwriters Guide to Collaboration, Revised and Expanded Second Edition
Critical Listening and Auditory Perception
Keyfax Omnibus Edition
The AudioPro Home Recording Course
Modular Digital Multitracks: The Power User's Guide
Concert Sound
Sound for Picture
Music Producers
Live Sound Reinforcement

Also from EMBooks:

Making the Ultimate Demo
Tech Terms: A Practical Dictionary for Audio and Music Production
Making Music With Your Computer

Also from CBM Music and Entertainment Group:

Recording Industry Sourcebook
Mix Reference Disc
Mix Master Directory
Digital Piano Buyer's Guide

MixBooks is a division of Cardinal Business Media Inc.
Printed in Auburn Hills, Michigan
ISBN 0-918371-11-2

Dedication

For Florence, my mother,

who taught me not only the importance of words

but also of finding the right ones.

Contents

Acknowledgments

My heartfelt thanks go to my sister Solange, whose professional editing skills and unflagging support helped to turn an idea into book.

Many thanks are also due to Jenn Schreiner, who helped to type and correct my manuscript, and to my family, friends, and business associates, whose help, advice, and suggestions were of immeasurable value.

I would also like to thank Mike Lawson and Lisa Duran of Cardinal Business Media, whose positive outlook and good advice gave me valuable insight on this work.

Introduction

This book is about how a musician or musical group can most efficiently use their time in a recording studio through a better understanding of the roles and responsibilities of the people involved.

A short time ago, I was reflecting on the last twenty years or so that I have spent in various recording studios large and small, and I began recalling all the blunders and gaffs that I had heard of, witnessed, been a part of, or (gasp!) caused. Two things came to mind. The first was that I consider myself very lucky to have continued to find opportunities in professional audio, and the second was that most of the bad stuff I saw or heard of in recording studios was caused by lack of knowledge. Sometimes the knowledge lacking was technical, but just as often the information lacking was what to do, when to do it, and who should be doing it. I realized that the overriding lesson I have learned is that the people involved with a session are more important than the equipment used in producing a sterling recording.

This may seem obvious to some, but I am not basing this opinion on the raw talent of the individuals involved. Artists and studio personnel can have all the talent in the world, but if they do not understand each other's point of view and work towards a mutual goal, it all will be for naught.

I have seen extremely talented musicians have frustrating experiences in recording studios because the studio staff wanted to impose their idea of what should happen on the artists rather than listen to their vision. I have also seen highly capable and understanding engineers and producers, in the most modern recording facilities, not be able to give their best because an artist could not organize or direct their part of the session. The people on either side of the control room glass need to understand and work with those on the other side.

This also seems obvious. Why does it not happen more often? The answer is twofold and deceptively simple. First of all, artists, engineers, and producers have a tendency to concentrate on what they do at the expense of what others are doing. To be sure, most engineers and producers have at least some experience playing music, but their focus is on the control room. Musicians have hundreds of hours under their belts practicing their parts but probably much less time running pro audio gear and marshalling their energies, as a group or singly, in a recording studio.

These realities led to the second, and most surprising, part of my realization. There was an information gap. This in the age of the information superhighway! There seemed to be an endless stream of publications to explain the mysterious inner workings of the latest and oldest electronic gadgets, reams of paper about transistors, faders, echo, microphones, reverb, diodes, speakers, recorders, MIDI, guitars, amplifiers, keyboards, acoustics, cables, computers, capacitors, and on and on, without a single tome dedicated to understanding the roles of the people involved in running all that stuff. The people! The people are what make a recording session fly or crash.

I searched far and wide and could find no volume dedicated to explaining the duties of the various players in a typical recording session. I spoke with many studio rats of all persuasions and experience levels, and all seemed to agree that a book dealing with this subject would be very useful to a lot of folks. The words I heard most often were, "I wish something like that had been on the market when I started." I began to understand that many people have learned by the seat of their pants how to choose and organize the best people for their recording sessions. I have learned much in the recording business through experience, but I must say that learning by making mistakes is the hardest and most time-consuming way to wisdom. Forewarned is definitely forearmed, and possessing some basic knowledge of the process of recording sessions will help you to spend less time, and money, in the studio getting exactly what you want.

I am, by necessity, making some assumptions in this book. It would be impossible to detail all the possible situations that could be encountered in recording sessions due to the infinite variety and scope of projects undertaken. I am writing so that both beginners and experienced professionals may gain some new understanding. I must assume that the great majority of people reading this work will not be working with million-dollar budgets and are embarking on a musical project of some kind. Even if you have a larger than usual budget or are involved in recording something other than music, the basic principles will still apply. I use the point of view of the artist, but studio personnel can use the same information to help their clients run their sessions better. I have avoided the explanation of technical matters as much as possible. There are many fine books explaining all the knobs and buttons, and tech stuff is not the subject of this book.

I wanted the reader to be taken through the process from beginning to end. Some sections, most notably Chapter 7, are meant as overviews only. I included these because I felt that ignoring them completely would be to deny their importance to the project. The subject of copyright protection alone is complex enough for its own book. I have included a section of selected titles that provide more detailed information on subjects far too complex to be covered by other than specialists in those fields, as well as a glossary of commonly used terms.

No matter how the technology of recording will change, the process of the recording session will remain basically the same. Artists will still try to transcribe what they hear in their heads onto a reproducing medium of some sort. Studio personnel will try to get the artist's vision to exist within the limits of the technology. These two principles are the driving force behind this book. I hope that all who read it will gain some new insight into the world where you are allowed to make as much noise as you want.

Chapter 1

Getting
Ready

WHY RECORD?

Because you are a creative genius, that's why! The world and all of humankind will be unfulfilled and less joyous for the lack of your particular brand of wheezing, groaning, and scratching.

There may still be a musical artist hiding somewhere in a corner of this planet who considers recording their work to be an unnecessary or unaffordable luxury. I don't know who they might be, but I do know that they are definitely wrong! Recording has become an essential part of advancing one's career and creative development.

The reasons for making a recording are numerous, but your reasons for making a particular recording should be outlined before undertaking any other steps, because all other decisions will be colored by the basic reasons you started this madness in the first place. If you think that you only want a three-song demo to send to agents and managers, your decisions regarding budget, studio, songs, in fact, every aspect of the project, may be radically different from a decision to record a commercial release-quality album for sale to a record company as a finished piece.

Your reasons for making a recording may be personal or you may be with a group who has decided to enter the studio. Either way, if you sit down and decide what you expect the recording to do, you will have a much better chance of getting there when it is done. Taking notes is a really good idea. I will probably repeat this note-taking business a lot, but I find notes to be invaluable. We all think that we will remember the salient points of a conversation, meeting, or even a discussion with ourselves, but sadly this is not the case. I say sadly because life would be so much easier if we all had video recorders running in our heads all the time with the capability of instant playback. There would be far fewer situations where one party swears they said they wanted pepperoni and a second party says they remember nothing of the request.

To avoid the stinging rebukes these confrontations commonly produce, I suggest taking notes. In fact, I suggest starting a notebook dedicated to nothing but your recording project. Unless you are looking to impress someone, fancy Dayrunners with leather covers are not necessary. A standard, spiral-bound, drugstore special should do the trick.

A notebook with dividers is a good idea so you can categorize your information. Keeping track of rehearsals could fill one section. As you begin to have specific rehearsals leading up to your recording sessions, keeping a log of rehearsals will give you a good idea of how much progress you are making and, later, how many hours were put in and by whom. Each rehearsal could have a page dedicated to it with the date, place, names of those participating, and the songs rehearsed, including comments on how the songs are coming along. If you are rehearsing with the same people in the same place every time, then keeping track of the place and participants is less important than if you are using hired players in a rented rehearsal studio. A record of songs rehearsed and comments is useful to any group, as it will help you to remember which parts of which songs need the most work.

Another section of your project notebook could be information gathered in your search for the perfect recording facility. The times, dates, what facilities were called, who you spoke to, and about what are all very useful details to write down as the information comes to you. Even if you are considering only one studio, the amount of information you will begin to collect can quickly become overwhelming. If you are talking to more than one studio, taking notes becomes essential. There will simply be too many details coming your way for you to remember them all. Dedicate at least one page to each recording studio with which you communicate.

Your budget and all monetary matters pertaining to your recording project is another good classification to keep separate. Once you start to get quotes on how much the services you need will cost, having them all organized in one section will help immeasurably with getting your budget nailed down. Make separate sections within the budget pages of your project notebook to keep track of quotes from the vendors or service providers in the various categories of your expenses (for categories, see "Budgeting Your Project" later in this chapter). Make a section under Budget for money actually spent. Get and keep receipts for all money spent.

Money actually spent is quickly and easily kept track of if you create pages that have headings with categories. They might look like this:

DATE	PAID TO	DESCRIPTION	AMOUNT
7/12/96	Jim's Taxi	Go See XYZ Studio	$11.75
7/13/96	BBT Rehearsal	3 hrs. rehearsal	$45.00
7/13/96	Fred T.	Sax, 3 hrs. rehearsal	$30.00

Your pages should have at least these categories and could have several more. You might want to keep a running total of how much has been spent to date. If the money for your project is coming from different sources, you would want to keep track of who paid for what. You might also want to keep track of what form of payment has been made (i.e., cash, check [with number], money order, cigars, live chickens, whatever). When it comes to money, the more detailed the records kept the better. You will never have to wonder how much has been spent and where it has gone if you keep good records.

Start a phone book section in your notebook. All the names, addresses, and phone numbers of the myriad of people and businesses you will be communicating with will probably fill several pages. It is a lot easier to find the numbers you need if they are all organized in one section rather than scattered all over your book or, worse yet, on little scraps of paper scattered all over your life. I know this for a fact as I am probably the little-scrap-of-paper king of the Western world. I have heard of a man in Sumatra who has more notes on scraps of paper than I, but I don't believe it. Even though I may generate a lot of scraps, I have trained myself to transfer the information into organized notebooks. This saves me from going nuts while looking for an important note.

One other section of your notebook should include your reasons for recording. Do you want to be able to sell your finished product? Do you expect to try and get radio airplay? Do you want to send your tape around to try and get live engagements (known to hip musicians as gigs)? Do you want to use your recording to try and impress industry types, booking agents, managers, record companies, etc.? Are you going to use the tape mainly as a giveaway to get publicity? These are some of the most common reasons musicians begin recording projects, but there could be many others that I cannot predict. The important thing is to delineate your reasons. If you do this, your decision-making process for the other parts of your scheme will become easier. Letting other participants down the road, such as a producer or engineer, know of your expectations will give them a much better shot at giving you what you want. This is very important. If you let a producer know that you are expecting to make a three-song demo for publicity purposes and possibly as a tool to get gigs for your band, they will have a good framework in which to place your project.

If you are part of a group, have a meeting and find out what the other members expect. This is particularly important if the recording is to be paid for by all members of the group. If each member feels that he or she is being heard and their desires taken into account, there is far less chance for disagreement down the road. This does not mean that all points of view can necessarily be satisfied, but at least you will know what all the others are thinking. The other people may actually have thought of things that you have not considered. Take notes and try to come up with the absolutely most important reasons why you are thinking of entering a studio. It will help later.

Ego gratification. This is one of the most common and best reasons to enter a recording studio. There is, I believe, no musician who, in at least some small part of their soul, does not want to hear their voice or instrument sparkling out of a pair of speakers, convincing themself and all the world of their undeniable talent. I do not believe that it is possible to make any really good art without a whacking great spoonful of ego thrown in. Just wanting to hear what you or your band sounds like on tape is one excellent reason to record. Even if you have no further plans to conquer the world with your killer new sound, making a reasonably good tape of your noise is a good idea. Besides, you never can tell what might happen. If your quickie tape were accidentally to fall into the hands of Ron Cashmycheque at MegaBucks Music and he called you up offering a recording contract, how many of you would say no?

Industry types. Managers, agents, record company A&R reps—they all want to hear a tape. If they didn't have demos to reject all day long, what would make them happy? Without sarcasm, a musical act is dead meat these days without some kind of recording. The first thing that anyone in the music business, from the owner of a corner pub to Mr. Cashmycheque, will ask you after you say you have a band is, "Do you have a tape?" If you are thinking of doing anything with your music other than playing for friends and family, you will have to make a recording. The music industry makes its bread and butter selling recordings. Some world-famous artists may make millions from touring, but the majority of acts barely break even playing live gigs. Aside from liking to play in front of people, most bands tour to support their current recording contract or in the hopes of getting one. Everyone in the industry will have a warm place in their hearts for a band that can not only play and write good songs but knows their way around a recording studio as well. You can prove this by making decent recordings before approaching industry types.

Radio stations. Radio stations play music. Almost all of this music is recorded. An all live-performance radio station might be fun but very hard to organize. Since radio stations play recorded music, they need endless supplies of the stuff. Most big commercial radio stations have very narrow play lists and will only play recordings released by major labels, but there is also a huge market for independently released music at smaller and college radio stations. Even some big stations have special time slots for homegrown talent. There is a really good chance that if you make a recording, someone, somewhere will want to play it on the air. How can this be bad?

Portability. This is a great reason to record. A tape is a lot easier to move than your band or even yourself. If there is someone across the country, or even across town, who would like to hear what it is that makes you so great, it is a lot simpler to send a tape. The ability to send little copies of yourself all over the place is one of the marvelous advantages of modern recording mediums. Tapes and CDs travel very well when properly packed and can turn people whom you could never afford to go see on to your music.

Whether your reasons include the above or you just have the itch to hear what you sound like, getting your reasons in order will smooth your path to recording success.

I find that having a notebook dedicated to every project I undertake to be essential. All the phone numbers, notes, dates, costs, and any other info you collect along the way is conveniently in one place and easy to transport. You will be able to keep track of what is happening. This is important. More projects go off the rails because of confusion than because of all other reasons combined.

You will also find that you are building an important catalog of resources and contacts that will help you in the future. A year down the road you may want to get hold of that sax player who blew such a ripping solo on your current recording, and you will be able to find the number quickly and easily by referring to your project notebook. Everyone involved in the recording business, artists and studio personnel alike, can benefit from having a well-organized system of contacts and resources.

CHOOSING SONGS

Choosing which songs or pieces will be recorded is a vital part of having a well-run session. You would really be surprised how many times I have seen bands get all set up in studios only to have one member say, "OK, what should we play?" Unless you have the money to use a recording studio as a hangout, this shouldn't happen.

Your choice of songs will largely be dictated by your budget and what you hope to accomplish with the completed recording. I know of many artists who decide to record just one tune because they only wanted to hear what a finished version sounded like or because that was all they could afford. This is fine. Just because you are in a recording studio does not mean you should be trying to record the maximum number of songs in the time you have. In most cases quite the opposite is true. Concentrating on fewer pieces will yield better results on the finished songs. Now, this doesn't necessarily mean that if you are planning to release a cassette with six songs on it that you must record only six songs. You may have the budget to be able to record eight songs and decide to use the ones that turn out best.

I will assume that most readers of this book will have quite limited budgets and subsequently not have the luxury to record material which may not be useful later. No problem. You just have to be a little more choosy when deciding what to record. Try and envision what you would like your finished product to be and do for you. If your band has ten original songs and you want to end up with a three-song demo that best shows off the band, you would do well to decide which three songs do that. If one of the songs you choose is your twenty-minute version of "Witchcraft" but you decide to leave off the three-minute song all your friends say they like, you might want to think again. Most acts would do well to factor in their audience's opinions when deciding what to record. The members of the group should also have a say, but they may be prejudiced because they like what they get to do in a particular song.

Perspective is one of the things you should seek when deciding which songs to record. That means listening to what other people have to say about your work and tempering your judgment accordingly. Audiences, club managers, and other musicians can all provide valuable insight. One of the best people to listen to is your producer if you can get them involved at this early stage of the game. A producer should be able to give you unbiased advice on what might turn folks on the most about what you do. None of this, though, means that you should go against your feelings about your own work. If you really think your newest tune is the most radically best thing ever written, then maybe you should include it. Remember, though, what seems like genius today can turn into tomorrow's "what was I thinking?" There is a lot to be said for being true to your own ideals, but if one takes too much of a screw-'em-that's-what-I-wanted approach, it is always possible that the rest of the world will decide that they don't want what you want. Listen to others, but always be true to yourself.

Choosing the songs that you will record will allow you and/or your group to concentrate on those songs during the rehearsals immediately preceding the sessions. Having a clean idea of which songs you want to record will help greatly in budgeting your project. I will get into these subjects more deeply in following sections.

REHEARSING TO RECORD

One could easily think that a rehearsal is a rehearsal, and if a performer or group can play their music to their satisfaction live, that they are ready to record. This is not always the case. Knowing some special rehearsal techniques prior to recording can help artists avoid being surprised by what the sensitive equipment in the studio picks up.

The modern recording studio is a super critical environment. The old expression of "Garbage in, garbage out" becomes more and more true as audio equipment becomes more able to reproduce all the subtleties, details, and nuances of performances. Along with picking up everything you are doing right, what you may be doing wrong will also be unerringly recorded. The best equipment in the world cannot make up for an artist's lack of preparation. There is no place for sloppy playing to hide in the recording studio. I am certain that neither you nor any member of your group play in anything other than angelic tones, but let's talk about looking for bugs anyway.

When rehearsing to record, concentrate on the songs you will be recording. Have special rehearsals to play those songs only. If you are writing new material, rehearsing for gigs, or just jamming, make those sessions separate from your recording rehearsals. In this way, the whole group can approximate the atmosphere of the recording studio. Try and keep distractions during these rehearsals, like friends hanging around, to a minimum. This will also help the players concentrate on what they are trying to do. Persons that find it hard to concentrate in rehearsal will find that the same habits work against them in the recording studio.

Everybody overplays. Most musicians come up through the ranks straining to do something that will excite an audience while having to deal with less-than-perfect instruments, amplifiers, and stage sound. We also all love the sound of our own part over all others. This leads to the very common and understandable tendency to overdo it. In terms of recording, less is definitely more. Listen very carefully to the arrangements of your songs. The arrangement means who plays what and when do they play it. Make sure that everything being played is absolutely necessary to the overall sound of the piece. Try having each member of your group play their part as sparsely as possible. Go as far as having each instrument play single notes instead of automatically playing chords. Build back up from there. See what effect this has on your pieces. It may sound kind of strange and empty, but this has a particular purpose. In the modern multitrack studio, it is quite easy to add more stuff. It is quite a different matter to try and remove all kinds of unwanted notes and scratchings from a track once it has been recorded. If you enter the recording process playing the bare bones of your songs, it will always be possible to add the other stuff if you find you want it. You may find that you don't.

If you have songs or sections of songs that you or your band find difficult to play well consistently, work on those songs or parts until they are solid. If a certain change or rhythm in a song is always shaky, repeat that part again and again until it gels. If a section does not seem to be getting steadier with rehearsal, it might be time to think about changing it. The part might be slightly beyond the capabilities of those playing or just might be unwieldy in a musical sense. Try making the part simpler and see if it still works for the song. Ask the players involved if there is some way the parts could be made easier for them. Some things just don't work well on certain instruments. If your guitarist is always complaining that a certain chord is difficult to manage consistently, try to find a chord that is easier to play but still has the same musical effect. It will also be possible to drop in that chord on tape during overdubs. Getting stuck having to repeat something over and over in a recording studio is an expensive and frustrating prospect. Go into the studio knowing your parts cold.

It is possible to mimic some of the playing situations you might encounter in the studio without needing expensive professional recording gear. Almost everyone has a cassette recorder of some kind that can be used to record rehearsals. A typical boom box will do quite nicely. Most boom boxes have built-in microphones, but for our purposes, the kind with separate inputs for microphones, left and right, is best. A home cassette deck can also be used as long as you can plug a pair of microphones into it. You don't need anything fancy for microphones; Radio Shack cheapies, ten or fifteen dollars each, are fine. Tell the counter person what you want them for and what you will be plugging them into. Purchase the ones you can best afford that are compatible with your equipment. If you can afford a pair of hundred dollar mics, please feel free to buy and use them. Better fidelity will only make it easier and more pleasurable to listen to your rehearsal tapes. With your stereo cassette recorder and two microphones, you are now set up to do some special recording while rehearsing. I can say with complete confidence that the more experience an artist has using recording equipment of any kind, the better prepared they will be for their foray into a professional recording studio.

If, like many musicians these days, you own a home multitrack recorder, usually 4- or 8-track on cassette, you can use these machines to great effect during your rehearsals. You may want to consider buying a home 4-track cassette recorder, along with a good book on home multitracking, to use during your rehearsals prior to your sessions in a pro studio. Even the inexpensive versions of today's home multitrack recorders are quite good at what they do.

If you choose to purchase and use a home multitrack machine for your rehearsals, buy a simple but good guide to its use (see RESOURCES chapter, "Further Reading"). The manufacturer's instructions are usually pretty good but can leave big holes in their advice for real world usage. Develop a relationship with the store as well as the salesperson that sold you the machine. They should be willing to give you advice on its use later on down the road. This type of advice is more likely to be available from the personnel in a store specializing in musical equipment than the average appliance store.

All the techniques described in this section having to do with making special recordings of rehearsals can be achieved more easily and possibly with better sound quality on a home multitrack recorder. There is such a variety of home multitrack machines and great operating guides available, that any attempt by me to describe their use in rehearsal recording would be redundant, so I will focus on techniques for stereo cassette recorders from this point on. However, all these operations can be transferred to multitrack recorders with great ease.

Whether using a home multitrack machine or the average "boom box," all those embarking on a recording project can gain valuable insight and experience by using audio recorders during their rehearsals.

The ability to repeat a section of music exactly as it was played earlier in the piece is a very important skill. Most popular music consists of sections of music played in a certain order and repeated at least once during a song. I am not trying to lock anyone into a particular style of playing or give rules for music, but what makes most people's toes tap when they hear a song is tight and consistent playing. Being sure of your parts and being able to play, for instance, a chorus of a song with the same power and confidence each time it comes up will go a long way toward making your songs sound as good as they possibly can. It will also reduce the amount of time needed to clean up the parts on tape.

There is one other reason, specific to recording, that being able to play a part exactly the same way each time is important. That reason is a common recording studio technique called doubling. To double a part, a performer will be asked to repeat a section of the music, instrument, or vocal while listening to the original track. The second run-through of the part is recorded on a separate track from the first. When played back together, the two tracks form a doubled part, and the sound of the voice or instrument is bigger and more present than any one track alone. No electronic device on the market today can fully reproduce the effect that true doubling has on a track. The best doubled parts are those that are perfectly coordinated. To achieve this, the second version of a part must be played or sung in exactly the same way as the first. When a doubled part is well-synchronized, it can be a beautiful thing. When you can hear ragged edges where the two performances do not exactly match up, the effect can be awfully amateurish.

Listen carefully to Kurt Cobain's vocals on Nirvana's recording of "Smells Like Teen Spirit." The effect of a doubled vocal part can be heard in the song's chorus sections. (The verses are not doubled but the choruses are.) Even though the singer is singing much louder and in a different register than on the verses, the striking change in the recorded sound of the vocal is achieved through doubling.

One of the most proficient artists I have ever heard in the technique of vocal doubling is Stevie Wonder. Many of his recordings feature doubled vocal parts performed so seamlessly that only the sound of the part gives away the trick to the trained ear. Every band wanting a huge guitar sound (Soundgarden is a good modern example) uses doubling methods when recording these instruments. Once you know what to listen for, you will hear this common effect on many other recordings, in virtually all styles of music, going all the way back to the first multitrack recordings of the 1950s.

Performers who are experienced with recording studios have probably had some experience with doubling tracks. Unless they are old pros at doubling, everyone who is going to perform on the recording will find they are better prepared if they practice the technique at home. This can be done with your trusty stereo cassette recorder. Set up a metronome or have your drummer play the beat for a particular song, and record this on one track, left or right, of a cassette. Then record the performer playing or singing their part on the other track at the same time. If both parts are being recorded with microphones, try to physically separate the mics as much as possible to achieve the greatest audio separation possible. Separation, in this case, means having no other sounds on a track other than those you choose to be there.

Let's say that you are recording an amplified instrument on one track and a drum set on the other track, and both instruments are in the same room. The sounds of the drum set will leak into the mic, picking up the sounds of the amplifier and vice versa. The easiest, cheapest, and least technically challenging way to deal with this problem is to physically isolate the smaller of the two sound sources. Find a heavy blanket, old curtain, or other such item and drape it completely over the amplifier and its mic. This technique serves two purposes: It prevents much of the amp's sound from getting into the room and, consequently, the drum mic, and it prevents most of the drums' sounds from reaching the amplifier mic.

If you are recording two acoustic instruments in the same room, you should have the performers sit as far away from each other as possible and place your mics as close to the instruments as is practical. The distance and close mic placement will provide better separation than if the instruments and mics are close together. If you are recording a piano on one track and a mechanical metronome on the other track, try putting the metronome on a table away from the piano, with the metronome's mic under a box and a blanket over the whole thing. If the metronome is sitting on the piano, where most people put one for rehearsing, you will never be able to separate the sounds.

At this point, you can very easily see a problem developing with sound separation. With your trusty metronome banging away under a box five feet away from the piano you are pounding, *how in the Sam Hill do you hear the beat?* Use your head...phones. There are very few cassette machines that do not have a headphone jack. If any budding Gershwin has their tape machine on the table behind them, they can plug a pair of headphones into its jack and "monitor," or listen to, the sound the metronome mic is picking up under the box while they are playing the piano. Many cassette machines only activate the headphone jack when the machine is in the record mode. If you wish to practice without actually recording, put the machine in record and pause.

If your mics are set up and plugged in, your machine is in the record mode, the recording level is properly set, and you have your headphones on, you will hear the sounds that both mics are picking up. If you are the piano player described above, you might not want to hear the amplified sound of the piano in your headset. You can't turn the record level down, because that would stop or decrease the signal sent to the tape. What to do? Slip the side of the headphones that has the piano in it to one side of your ear. If that proves uncomfortable, you can try pulling the plug one click out of the headphone jack. If it is the metronome that stops when you do that, reverse the mic cords in the inputs. The metronome should reappear. If it doesn't, gently push the headphone plug into the jack until you hear the sound.

You may find it useful to monitor your recordings with headphones even if no separation problem exists. Many performers find it useful to hear what the tape recorder is hearing while making recordings. Some find wearing headphones distracting. Whether you like the "phones" or not, getting used to playing while wearing them is a good idea. The chances are very high that you will have to do at least some recording with headphones on.

It is impossible for me to try and predict every different type of recording situation you may encounter while making your rehearsal tapes. Neither can I know, specifically, what type of recording equipment you might be using. The above examples were given to illustrate that a lot can be done to get acceptable results without breaking your bank or standing on your head trying weird setups. When making your tapes, use your imagination to get the best results.

In general, I can advise you not to spend too much time trying to make really great sounding recordings while rehearsing. The sonic quality will be provided by the recording studio. Concentrate on producing useful tapes that will help the participants perfect their parts and making the parts suit the songs as if fitted by a master tailor.

With this tape and a home stereo, an instrumentalist or singer can play or sing along with themselves and concentrate on having the performances match up. By using the left/right balance control of the stereo, one can adjust the volume balance between the rhythm and the melody part.

One of the most unnerving situations that musicians confront while recording is being asked to sit in a room alone and play their parts while listening to a click track (electronic metronome) or previously recorded parts. It is very easy to feel strange, out of place, and in the spotlight in this circumstance, especially if most of your experience has been onstage or in rehearsal. Using your home equipment can help you get used to this strange state of musical loneliness.

Have a rehearsal session for the specific purpose of making "minus one" versions of your songs. These are recordings in which one or more instruments are purposely not played so as to be missing on tape. The member of the group whose instrument is missing can take the tape home and practice playing along with it. This will approximate the feeling of overdubbing tracks in a studio and will give the musician the ability to hear what they are doing in greater detail than when they are playing with the band. Try making separate tapes of each song with one instrument out in front (louder) than the others. One tape might feature the bass player out front, another would be made with the keyboards louder than anyone else, and so on. This can be accomplished by putting your microphones or boom box closer to and facing the instrument you want to highlight. You could also have all the other members of your band play a lot quieter than the featured instrument. Listening to the result will give the featured player a very good idea of how successfully they are playing their part. I have found that a well- written and well-played part sounds good all by itself. If it doesn't, now is the time to change or fix it.

In many forms of popular music, the coordination of the bass and drums are pivotal to getting a solid sound behind a song. While making your "minus one" rehearsal tapes, I would strongly suggest taping a special version of your songs with the bass and drums way out front or even playing without the rest of the band. Having your bassist and drummer perform these special versions of your material will serve two very important purposes. First, they will get valuable experience in performing the songs without hearing all the other instruments and vocalists. They may be required to do just this in the recording studio, because many multitrack recordings start by recording the bass and drums alone, or with sparse accompaniment, and then the other parts are layered, or overdubbed, over the rhythm section. If your bass player and drummer have never done this before, it may be kind of strange for them. Practicing their parts this way will give them added confidence if they are asked to perform in the same manner when recording.

The other purpose to taping the rhythm section alone is to be able to listen closely and critically to the parts they are playing. Doing this will surely turn up any glitches that may have been hiding in the overall arrangement of the song. If the bass and drums are not tight, then the song cannot be.

After you have gotten your songs as tight as you want and have your parts worked out and practiced, record yourself or your group all together with your trusty boom box or cassette deck. True, these machines do not give the best sonic quality when placed in the middle of a rehearsal room, but I have found most of them to be sensitive and accurate enough to give you a decent reflection of how a group sounds. Make a test recording. Try putting the mics or boom box in different positions in your rehearsal room. Place the recorder where it is picking up all the instruments and vocals as evenly as possible. When you listen to these recordings, do not expect great sound quality. It won't be there. What you, and your producer if you have one, are looking for is overall performance. Are all members doing what is necessary to make the piece as a whole really cook? If the right feel of the performance does not consistently show up on rehearsal tapes, I strongly suggest trying to identify what the problems are and fixing them now, rather than expecting the recording studio to magically provide something in the performance that is not there. I find that a group that really grooves will do so on almost any type of recording. Obviously a good recording studio will be able to do all sorts of things to make your music special, but if someone in the group can't cut the changes or the arrangement of the tune isn't successful, no amount of dial twisting will make those things very much better.

Many producers and engineers use click tracks when recording to ensure an even and consistent tempo over the course of a song and between different takes of the same song. Playing along with a click track takes some getting used to for even the most time-accurate of musicians. Since drums are usually used to drive the beat of modern music, most often it will be the drummer who will be asked to listen to, and coordinate his or her playing with, the click track while recording. This involves wearing headphones with an electronic click playing through them. The speed and volume of the click can be adjusted to suit.

There are several types of inexpensive electronic metronomes on the market today that can perform the duties of a click generator for the purposes of rehearsal. Get one that has a jack for sending the click signal to an amplifier or tape recorder. Connect the metronome to an amplifier that can feed a set of headphones, and set this up for your drummer where you rehearse. It is much easier for a drummer to hear a click track through a set of headphones than through a speaker playing into a room. The salesperson at the music store where you purchase your metronome should be able to help explain how to hook this up. Your drummer can also practice playing with a click track by listening to a beat from a drum machine. Set the drum machine to play a snare hit or other simple sound on beats 2 and 4, and you will have an approximation of what a click track in a studio will sound like. Connect the drum machine to an amplifier that can drive a set of headphones and away you go.

Don't assume that the other musicians who will play on your session will not benefit from practicing their parts with a click track. They will. Make a cassette tape of your click track for each member of your band, so they can rehearse their parts at home with the click. Playing alone with only a simple, unwavering beat really shows how well you have mastered a musical part.

Some musicians, especially drummers, may feel that being asked to play with a machine setting the tempo is a slight to their time-keeping abilities. This is not so. Many technical aspects of modern recording are made less problematic if the tempo of a musical piece is consistent and predictable. No human being has the ability to set an exact one hundred twenty-two beats per minute tempo, or any other tempo, and keep it precisely set over the course of a song, every time. Click tracks merely help musicians achieve a measure of consistency not possible without them. It is not true that all forms of music benefit from, or require, the use of click tracks. If you are unsure if you will be using a click track during your session, consult your producer or the recording studio staff.

Don't over rehearse. Even though you and your compatriots need to get prepared to record, you don't want to go too far and have everyone involved really sick of playing the tunes. One of the most important and intangible things that make recordings really good is the enthusiasm that the artists pour out in the studio. Don't drain that all away by pushing yourself or the others too hard. This is a fairly mushy area. Knowing when people are so tired of doing something that no good work is being done is particular to the people and the situation. I recommend that your heavy rehearsals stop a few days prior to the sessions and that you do a light brush up a day or two before recording. That way everyone should know their parts well and still be fresh and ready to play. Ask your players to listen a lot to the tapes made in rehearsal. Really knowing the songs well is key to being able to tear through one great take after another. Going into the recording studio well-rehearsed will allow you to avoid that sinking feeling you get when you hear the engineer's bored voice say, "OK, guys. Take number fourteen."

BUDGETING YOUR PROJECT

Only a few years ago, I would have had to admit that a professional sounding recording would cost the average musician or band quite a bit more than a bagger at the local supermarket could afford. Happily for modern minstrels, this is no longer the case. Even though many of the songs heard on the radio, in major movies, and on television still cost piles of dough to produce, the equipment used in audio recording has advanced to the point of making professional quality audio affordable to all but the most impoverished of strummers and warblers. That doesn't mean that you can get the New York Philharmonic to play for one hundred bucks, but you can get a reasonable facsimile.

Artists are making quite remarkable recordings with inexpensive equipment that did not even exist a few years ago, much less was available to the general public at affordable prices. There is a lot of audio recording gear on the market today that is aimed at the do-it-yourselfer. Many of these contraptions have sound quality and capabilities that get very close to, or meet, professional specs. Before I get into the details of budgeting a recording session in a commercial studio, I would like to look at another option. That would be to buy your own recording studio.

"Yeah, sure. I'll buy a limo to go with it," you might say. Don't be incredulous. It is quite possible to purchase a quality recording setup for what you might pay for one or two sessions in a commercial studio. Let's take a $3000 budget, for example. A very reasonable price for time in a hired 24-track studio would be $45 per hour. That would get you approximately sixty-six hours of time. Lots of time, right? Well, not if you want to produce versions of all thirteen of the best songs your band does. Your sixty-six hours of time would break down to slightly over five hours per song, and believe me, that is not a lot of time to give to recording a song. What if you feel like experimenting a little? You'd be lucky to get five songs finished in the time allotted. Once you have used up all your money in a rented studio, you are finished recording. Period. Want to go again? Come up with more cash.

The same $3000, if well spent, could buy a rig that might give you the type of sound you were hoping for. And you would still have the equipment to play with after your thirteen songs were done...as long as you pay the power bill. Sounds great. Let's go to the audio supermarket. Whoa, Nellie! There are a few things to be considered before deciding you don't need all those effete studio snobs with their fancy recording machines.

There are many drawbacks to trying to produce your own recordings on your own equipment. Do you know what to buy? There are thousands of products on the shelves. Do you know how to run the stuff? People spend years learning all the tricks of the trade. In many ways, there is simply no substitute for years of practical experience when it comes to audio recording. Can you afford all the audio gee-gaws you need to produce the type of recordings you want? Most people can't afford all the cool stuff that commercial studios have. Do you even know what you might need? Different types of equipment can either be very useful or almost useless for your particular recording project. Where are you going to be able to set up the equipment to use it? Your garage is probably not the best option. Professional recording studios spend oodles of time and even more money getting their rooms to sound good before they install the first mic stand. If the recording room sounds weird or is full of background noise like most garages or basements, it will be hell on wheels to try and record a solid-sounding project.

With all these questions, one can easily see that the do-it-yourself option is not a choice to be taken lightly. In fact, it is such a complicated option that there are literally dozens of books and video tapes for sale explaining all the details.

The best thing I can tell you in a short space is that if you are considering spending your budget on your own equipment, you would do well to educate yourself like crazy before making any decisions. Having your own recording gear can give you hours of family fun and the ability to experiment to your hearts content, or you could find yourself mired in a confusing mass of options. Consider the buy-your-own option, but consider it warily. There are lots of folks out there in the woods with their own recording systems, some of which are quite sophisticated and expensive, scratching their heads and wondering why it just never sounds right.

Let's say that you have decided not to try and build your own digital multitrack recording studio out of balsa wood and rubber bands. This means that you will be buying time on someone else's equipment. Whether you have $500 saved from your job at 7-Eleven or $50,000 from your dear Aunt Mabel—thanks Mabel!—you still have a finite amount of money to spend. The amount of money that can be spent on a project is the most limiting practical factor, hence the most important matter to consider before making any other plans.

There are two ways of making a budget for a recording session. The first is to decide how much money is available and then decide how to spend it. The second is to decide what you want, find out how much it costs, and then see if you can afford it. Either way, the easiest way to simplify the process is to create a budget sheet listing all the necessary session expenditures by category and the amounts to be spent on each. Such a plan might look like this:

Studio Time	$_____
Recording Tape	$_____
Musicians	$_____
Music Copying	$_____
Producer	$_____
Engineer/Assistant	$_____
Equipment	$_____
Duplication	$_____
Rehearsal	$_____
Transportation	$_____
Meals/Lodging	$_____
TOTAL	$_____

If this budget were created for our band with a fictitious $3000 limit, it might look something like this:

Studio Time (35 hrs. x $45 per hr.)	$1575
Recording Tape	$ 300
Musicians	$ ___
Music Copying	$ ___
Producer	$ 525
Engineer/Assistant	$ ___
Equipment	$ 200
Duplication	$ 500
Rehearsal	$ ___
Transportation	$ ___
Meals/Lodging	$ 150
TOTAL	**$3250**

Oops! Over budget. Not the first time this has happened with recording budgets. This band has two options: reduce their expenses or raise the extra $250. In the event of small overruns like this, less than ten percent, I would lean toward raising the extra money. Except for the $150 for meals/lodging, there appears to be very little fat on the budget. This band is rehearsing at home, is hiring no studio musicians, has not reserved limos, and reasonably expects to need thirty-five hours to record and mix their three-song demo. If this band has to stay overnight in a strange town to record, then I would say there is no fat and the amount over budget is small.

You might think that the $525 budgeted for the producer could be eliminated or reduced. Maybe. But in this case, the band is relying on their professional producer to get a polished sound out of a group of musicians with little or no studio experience. The producer has agreed to work for $15 per hour (a very reasonable rate) because he likes them and thinks they have promise. The band might propose a spec deal with the producer (see APPENDIX), but for this amount of money, they would do better to try to pay outright. For this band, in this situation, the route to take is to raise the extra dough.

If this same band had found their budget to be over budget by $1000, thirty-three percent, or more, then I would start to look at each category carefully and see where some cuts could be made. Does the third song really need the Bulgarian choir? Really? Do you have to stay in the most expensive hotel in town, eating only from room service? When session budgets go seriously over budget, there is almost always something that can be cut or reworked to help the project fit economic reality. Maybe the scope of the whole scheme needs to be rethought. Instead of trying to record an entire album's worth of material, perhaps the band should record fewer songs. For a demo project, do you really need a studio with 48-track capability? Even with larger budgets, you would be surprised how quickly too much money can be spent.

A lot of self-contained bands or solo performers will not have any expenses at all in some of these categories (as shown in the above budget), but I will describe all of them here. Let's take a look at them one at a time.

Studio time. This is the total amount of money required to buy the time necessary to complete your project. Include both recording and mixing time. Total time for a session is always an estimate, but this estimate can be loose or tight according to the amount and quality of the information passed between the artists, producer, and studio. This will be one of the largest money eaters in most session budgets. Extra session time can easily bust your budget. Get as tight an idea as possible of the amount of time you will need, and then add at least twenty percent to that figure to cover unforeseen circumstances. (For more on studio time, see Chapter 4, "Booking Time.")

Recording tape. There are no hard and fast rules as to how much of your budget this category will or should consume. Most of us are used to buying recording tape only as cassettes at the local Wal-Mart, and we see the cost as being negligible. Don't assume this about pro formats. Some types of professional recording tape are very expensive. The type of tape used on a studio's equipment can have an important effect on whether you can afford that studio or not.

Let's look at the most widely used multitrack formats. Many artists still prefer the sound of analog multitrack recorders, even though digital technology touts better specs. Most professional 24-track recorders use 2-inch wide tape on 10½-inch reels. A single 10½-inch reel of 2-inch wide tape for a 24-

track, analog, multitrack recorder can cost well over $150 per reel. When used at high speed, 30 ips (inches per second), which gives the best fidelity, this reel will record only fifteen minutes of program material. Even at a lower speed, 15 ips, the reel will only record thirty minutes of material. Since most recording sessions involve recording multiple takes of each selection, a half hour of recording tape can easily be eaten up recording just one or two songs. You can see how quickly fifteen, or more, reels of tape could be used to record an album's worth of material. Do the math. Fifteen reels of 2-inch tape at $150 per reel is $2250! We have not even considered the cost of the tape on which your mixes will be recorded.

Digital multitrack tape recorders, ADATs, and DA-88 recorders use tape that comes in cassettes with a cost of about $15 to $20 per cassette. These machines will record a half hour of program material at high speed. Sounds like a great deal. The only problem is that these machines record only eight tracks of material per machine and must be used in synchronized operation with matching machines to get more than eight tracks of multitrack recording. Thus, a studio using ADAT will have to operate four machines simultaneously with a separate cassette in each to achieve 24-track recording capability. This means that the cost for thirty minutes of 24-track recording tape is four times the cost of one cassette. Once again, this can get pretty pricey.

One more type of multitrack recording system that is gaining popularity is hard disk recording. This is a digital system that uses no tape at all. Whoopee! Not so fast. Hard disk recorders fix their program material onto an internal computer disk drive that is not meant to be removed from the machine to make the information portable. How do you get to take your recordings with you? You must dump the computer information to an outboard information storage system of some kind. If you want to make sure that you will be able to access your multitrack recordings at a later date, in a different facility, you will probably have to purchase an outboard storage system device to be sure of compatibility with another digital multitrack facility. These things, as you can guess, ain't cheap.

I'm not trying to numb you with the technical details of all this. It is safe to say that no system of multitrack recording will let you get off scot-free, or even cheaply, in terms of the cost of running a particular technology. You must do some investigating to get a good idea of how much it will cost you to run the machine in the studio you choose. The personnel in a studio, running a particular recording machine, are the best folks with whom to discuss these costs.

After weighing advice from your producer, engineer, and the studios you talk to, and then finding the best deal, you could easily be spending several hundred dollars or more for tape or disks alone. Be sure you have the firmest possible estimate of how much tape you will need and how much it will cost.

Musicians. Many sessions require the services of one or more hired musicians. They may be specialists in a particular style or play instruments not played by band members. Have a firm agreement with any hired performers, in writing is always a good idea, detailing what their services will be and what they will cost. Some players may give you one price for the whole session, others may quote an hourly rate. Whatever the case may be, figure the total cost and add it to your budget sheet.

If you are thinking of hiring musicians, personal recommendations from other players are always a good place to start. The studios you are talking to should be able to provide the names of players they have used for other projects. Local music schools or music equipment shops may be able to provide some leads. Do not overlook the American Federation of Musicians (see RESOURCES chapter, "Industry Associations") as a place to find real pros. AFM members will probably charge more than the "average Joe," but all truly professional musicians belong to this union.

In all cases, describe in the fullest detail possible what you are expecting of a hired musician and always ask what they expect to be paid. This way, your search will be shorter and have fewer frustrating, cold leads.

Music Copying/Arranging. Believe it or not, some musicians still play from written music. I know this is shocking, but it is true. If you have hired a horn section to play on your ultra funky tunes, chances are they will want to play their parts from written music known as "charts." Sometimes the musicians themselves will be able to write out their own charts, but you may have to hire a music copyist in the off chance that you can't scribble the notes out yourself. Unless you are hiring someone to tear off a killer impromptu solo, you will save a lot of studio time by having a chart for hired players.

Music copyists are becoming a rare breed in these days of computer-generated sheet music, but they definitely do still exist. If you have, or know someone who has, a computer program that will generate printed music after information has been entered via keyboard or step programming, you may be able to get good charts this way for your hired hands. Unfortunately, many computer programs are not as adept at transferring the nuances of musical performances to written form as well as old, trusty analog humans.

If you need to hire a music copyist and none of your friends know of one, the music school/college, music equipment shop, or AFM route should lead you to likely candidates.

While you are looking for a copyist, unless you have figured out note for note what you want your hired musicians to play, you may need to hire an arranger or designate one of them to be one. An arranger will take your idea for a song and fill out the accompaniment by deciding what instruments to use and what notes each instrument will play. Many arrangers also work as music copyists and vice versa.

If you hire an arranger, getting the right one for your project will have a huge effect on the outcome. Make sure that any prospective arranger knows what you are expecting, can afford, and will demonstrate for you what they are thinking of before you start hiring musicians and running into a studio.

Producer. This person will charge a fee to shepherd your project along. It will either be a flat fee or an hourly rate. You, a member of your band, a respected musical friend, or your engineer may be performing this duty either free of charge, or the engineer may include producing chores in their overall fee. (For more on producers, see Chapter 2.)

Engineer/Assistant. For twisting knobs and plugging things in, the engineer will receive a fee. In larger studios, it is necessary to have an assistant to keep from wasting the engineer's time running back and forth from the control room to the recording rooms. I have been involved in quite a few sessions where the presence of a knowledgeable assistant saved many hours of expensive studio time. Many times, the fee charged by recording studios for time includes the services of a house engineer. If so, this category is covered by "Studio Time." If not, or you have decided to use an independent engineer, enter the amount necessary to procure their services. (For more on engineers, see Chapter 3.)

Equipment. The equipment category should cover the purchase, rental, or repair of musical or technical items needed for your session. Technical items would include special audio processing gear or specific microphones your producer or engineer thinks are necessary. Musical items would be instruments, amplifiers, and accessories. (For more on equipment, see Chapter 1, "Your Equipment," and Chapter 4, "Studio Equipment.")

Duplication. This category covers the copying of your finished master tape. Your budget for reproduction should include mastering costs, graphics, actual duplication units (cassettes, CDs, etc.), and packaging. If you are going to be sending your copies out as a package with pictures, bios, and press clippings, include the cost of producing and reproducing the different parts of your package. Make sure to include the cost of posting your recording and various publicity items. (For more on duplication, see Chapter 6, "Release Formats/Duplication.")

Rehearsal. This category is for the cost of the rented rehearsal studio used by the performers to polish their parts before entering the recording studio. Some hired musicians may need to be paid to rehearse as well as play on the actual recording. (For more on rehearsing, see Chapter 1, "Rehearsing to Record.")

Transportation. Add up how much it will cost to get you and your performers and other participants to the sessions and rehearsals. For most bands, the individuals involved will be responsible for their own transportation, but this is far from always the case. Taxis, trucks, trains, airplanes, and gasoline all cost money. If your people need help with transportation costs, try and nail down how much. (For more on transportation, see Chapter 4, "Location.")

Meals/Lodging. This category will cover the costs of providing rooms for participants who may come from out of town and feeding the participants. If you or your band are traveling any distance to use a studio, this category cannot be ignored. Even for a session held in your town with all involved being local, there will be calls for coffee, doughnuts, pizza, or a celebratory beer after the session is done. (For more information, see Chapter 4, "Location.")

Figure into your budget how much travel, lodging, and meals will cost. It may be a considerable amount, but it may be worth it. The studio may be able to help you arrange a discount at a local hotel or motel. They might even be able to arrange free lodging. Once again, it doesn't hurt to ask.

For the great majority of people planning their first recording sessions or those facing limited budgets, many of these categories, indeed, even the idea of creating a detailed budget may seem superfluous. Even if you do not have expenses in all categories or your plans seem too simple to track the costs, I highly recommend that you create a written budget. It will help you keep costs in check and, when it is all done, will tell you where your money was spent. Knowing where the money went may help you with taxes later on. For lots of folks, their activities and expenses in music are tax deductible. Keeping detailed records helps you get your just desserts. Oh, yes. Ask for and keep all receipts!

YOUR EQUIPMENT

After at least forty-five minutes of re-patching (connecting electronics in different configurations), searching, and head scratching trying to figure out how to get rid of the hum that was showing up on his track, I asked the bass player to come into the control room. As soon as he heard what was vexing us and holding up the session for so long, he said, "Oh that? My bass has always done that. Once we start playing, you can't hear it." I am sure that he could see smoke coming from my ears as I quietly fumed. This person was aware that his equipment was not working properly and had not taken the trouble to get it fixed. You might think that you can get away with some rattle and hum onstage or in rehearsal, but in a recording studio you will hear it. You will hear it, and you will not like it.

Everyone who is performing on a recording should go into the studio with their instruments and amplifiers in tip-top shape. Everything that will be used should be checked and, if possible, spares should be brought along just in case Murphy's Law goes into effect. The session described above was brought to an abrupt halt until a spare instrument could be located and transported to the studio, because, of course, the bassist had not brought a spare with him.

Since most of us do not have all the money in the world to put into our instruments and equipment, we get used to living and working with them in less than perfect condition. OK, this is not a perfect world, but a special effort should be made when entering into special situations. You will have to live with the sounds that will be recorded during your session for a long time. Getting your gear into the best possible shape will allow you to play and sound your best.

If you play a stringed instrument (guitar or bass, maybe?) get your axe professionally set up. This includes buying a new set of strings; setting the action; setting the intonation; and on electric instruments, checking the pots and jacks. Setting the action properly could get rid of that annoying buzz you always get on the fourteenth fret. Setting the intonation properly ensures that your stringed wonder will stay in tune no matter where you play on the neck. Noisy pots or volume and tone controls can cause unwanted noise and unstable instrument output. Most full-service music stores can perform this service for about $30-40. It's well worth it.

New strings are a must even if your instrument has been recently set up to proper specs. New strings have the brightness, full overtones, and presence that most of us associate with a good-sounding instrument. They are also easier to play. I have heard of some bass players who swear by the set of strings they have had on their bass for five years. If you must use those old rubber bands, then I suppose you must. But I have never heard an instrument's sound that was not vastly improved by a new set of strings. Of course, you know to stretch them well before you actually start to record. Oh, yes. Bring at least one spare set with you to the session.

Drummers should also heed the new-strings admonition except that their strings are their drum heads. I have seen drummers bring in perfectly good drum sets from which they couldn't get a good sound, simply because the heads were so beat up. Even a few rehearsals will slam some of the life out of a set of heads. So a new set all around, just before the session, is a really good idea. If you can't afford a whole new set of heads, at least get a new snare head, as this is probably the most important sound in your set. Drum tuning is a delicate and misunderstood art. If you are not absolutely sure you can tune your set to perfection, I would recommend getting them professionally tuned before the session. Many a drum set sounds dead for lack of good tuning. Once again, a full-service music store should be able to do this for you. Go to the shop when they tune your drums. You will be able to approve the tones that are set, and you might even pick up some of what they do for the future.

Inspect the whole drum set. Make sure that all hardware and pedals are tight and as noise-free as possible. One of the biggest time wasters in recording sessions is the squeaky bass drum pedal. Most of the time this problem can be dealt with before the session. Lubricate all pedals with Vaseline. It's nice and thick and doesn't drip off. You can always wipe the goo off later if you want. Listen to each drum one at a time, and make sure there are absolutely no rattles or other noises you don't want. You will really be surprised how loud and annoying even a small buzz from a drum sounds when a very sensitive microphone is placed near it. If you are having trouble with metal-to-metal or metal-to-wood fasteners, try getting or making rubber or felt washers to put between the offending parts. If you can't find what you need in your local music store, try the plumbing section of a hardware store. In short, do whatever is necessary to shut up the noises!

Amplifiers are also prone to making unwanted sounds. Speakers should be firmly mounted in their cabinets, and the cabinets themselves should be checked to make sure that all fittings are tight and rattle-free. Of course, the electronics of the amp should be working properly before being brought into the studio. A recording studio is not a repair shop. Do not expect them to fix your stuff as part of the session. If your amp has problems, have it serviced by a professional before your recording date. And don't assume that this will be a one-day turnaround job. Many repair shops are backed up with work, and the parts for your rig may not be readily available. If your amp needs service, start the process well before the session. Suppose you find out that your beautiful 1963 Fender black-face Super Reverb needs more work than you can afford before the session. Well, maybe the studio can arrange a rental replacement. Of course, if you must have an exotic amp, it will be more difficult to arrange a replacement, but many studios have contacts for all kinds of rental equipment. If you don't think that your amps will make the grade, ask the studio what they might be able to provide or suggest. Do this well before your session.

These days, keyboard players have less to do in terms of making sure their instruments are in tune and such. They do have to make sure that all their sounds are programmed in a way so as to be easily accessible and that their whole rig works well consistently. If you are planning extensive control interfacing between your equipment and the studio's, I would suggest that your producer, keyboard player, and engineer have a meeting to discuss plans. Finding out beforehand how, and *if,* all the equipment will "talk" to each other will save a lot of time during the recording sessions.

I strongly suggest bringing the appropriate operation manuals to the session for any equipment that requires programming changes to vary its function. Even proficient users of program-driven devices may need to access areas of programming not normally used outside of recording studios. Make sure you bring all the program disks and MIDI cables necessary. AC adapters for keyboards and other accessories should be in good working order and not forgotten.

Accessories such as connection cables, effects pedals, straps, and your own rack mount stuff should all be checked and working well. That guitar cable or wah wah pedal that works fine most of the time is bound to screw up at two in the morning when you are locked in a recording studio. If your pedals are noisy or intermittent, get them serviced or replaced. If some of your cables are dicey, replace them. Make sure to bring enough of your own instrument connection cables. Don't assume that the studio has endless supplies of these. Cables with 1/4-inch phone plugs, commonly used to connect instruments and effects, are not used all that much in many studios, and they are not responsible for hooking up your equipment.

I cannot go through all the possible problems that could arise with all the instruments that may be used on your session. Suffice to say that you should alert all involved to get their stuff in shape. It is quite frustrating to have a sax player stop in the middle of a great solo because of a split reed only to find out that they didn't bring any spares.

Make a list. I know, here I go again with this list thing. But if you make a list of all the things you do not want to forget when you are actually leaving for the studio, chances are you won't. When your list is finished, you might be surprised at the number of items on it. If at all possible, bring spares or subs for everything. I know this may not be practical for large or expensive items, but it is a really good idea for all the small stuff. If you have two guitars, bring them both. Not only might one sound better than the other for a particular part, but if one goes south, you can just pick up the other one and keep smiling. This holds true for all the other stuff you might have spares for.

With all your tools in top shape, you are in a great position to put in your best performance. In fact, for most people, and I know it's true for me, if your paraphernalia is not in order, your tent will not go up. Go the extra mile to ensure that your contraptions go bang when you want them to and you will thank yourself later. Trust me. You might even thank me.

Oh, yes. Bring plenty of extra batteries.

Chapter 2

The Producer

When you think of a producer, do you get an image of a balding, fat man trying to get a starlet onto a casting couch in Hollywood? That may be an image fostered by film industry stereotypes, but it has little to do with producers in the recording industry. You've seen their credits on all the commercial recordings you own, but do you know what they do? Do you know how important they are? Do you know that you need one?

A producer is an absolutely essential part of the recording process. The next sections will explain why you need one, what they do, and who might make a good producer for your session.

THE PRODUCER'S ROLE

The Hydra, a multi-headed monster in Greek mythology, had no more heads than a good producer needs, and each one of those heads must wear several caps. The producer's role covers many areas of responsibility and requires skill and experience in many disciplines. The role of the producer of a recording is analogous to the role of the director of a film.

Then why not call that person the director? Sometimes things just don't work out that way. The term "producer" was used in theater and films to mean the person who, in simple terms, bankrolled a project and chose the director. The director made the film, and the actors acted. The producer, the person who held the purse strings, had the ultimate authority. In the early days of commercial recording, virtually no one could afford to record independently of a record company or a financial backer. Record companies and backers, the producers, wanted to have control over what their artists did with their expensive recording time and so appointed overseers. Many times these overseers were the record company executives or the backers themselves. So, it developed that any person in a recording studio who had the overall responsibility of seeing that the concept envisioned was successfully realized was called the producer.

The producer is the director. The producer makes decisions. Since there are usually several different points of view affecting a recording project, someone must decide which will take precedence. Will the sax be soft or loud? Will the guitar be distorted or clean? Will the backup singers sing "shoo wop" or "doo wop"? Reverb or delay or both on the drum set? Record on digital or analog machines? Use studio X or studio Y? Synthesizer or a real accordion? Plain socks or argyle? I think you get the idea.

Virtually any decision to be made about a recording session can end up in the producer's lap, and rightfully so. Someone has to make decisions. There are so many possibilities and variables in modern recording, the producer's role has become paramount. Many world-famous artists wouldn't think of entering a studio without the direction of a trusted producer. Bruce Springsteen refused to record for over two years when he was kept from working with Jon Landau as his producer because of legal problems.

Many producers are recognized as being responsible for getting truly great recordings out of their artists. Producer Roy Thomas Baker is given much of the credit for developing the unique sound that propelled Queen to world-wide success. The importance of having a good producer involved with a recording project cannot be overstated.

I believe that someone needs to take on the role of producer for any serious recording project. I have seen far too many potentially good recording sessions get mired in indecision and the end product becoming far less powerful and cohesive solely because nobody was sitting in the producer's chair. Most of the time this seems to happen because the importance of the producer is underestimated. Inexperienced artists think that because they do not have room in their budgets to hire an independent producer, they will do without. Neither of these situations should force a project to go to sea without someone at the helm.

By the time you are finished with this chapter, I hope that you realize the need to designate a producer. If you do not have the budget for independent help, you can self produce. Early in many careers, artists are forced to self produce or take the advice of persons who work for the studio in which they are to record. This can be just fine as long as the function of the producer is understood and not ignored. The most important attribute any producer will bring to a session is perspective. In this instance, perspective means the ability to view what is being done from all angles and to make judgments based on what is good for the overall success of the project.

Ideally, a producer will become involved in a project long before the first reel of tape is loaded in a recording studio. The producer could have input concerning which songs out of an artist's repertoire might be the best to record. They might sit in on rehearsals and make suggestions about arrangements and playing styles. A producer could suggest recording studios that they think will fit the needs and budget of the artist. The producer may prepare the studio staff for what the session is going to attempt. The producer will certainly oversee the recording and mix sessions, and after the project is finished they may act as a contact between the artist and the record companies and other music industry professionals. How much input a producer has and how deeply they get involved with a session is different with each producer and each session.

If you are going to be recording as part of a group, it is important that everyone in the group understands the importance of designating a producer and that they trust the person who is chosen. If the producer is a member of the group, that person should make sure that their decisions are based on the good of the recording and not play favorites. Decisions should not be made to service the egos of the artists at the expense of the recording. If the engineer for your sessions will be giving producing advice, it is important that the members of the group have at least one meeting with the engineer to discuss this. If a member of your group is going to take the role of producer, make sure that the other members appreciate that this person will be the decision maker during the recording sessions. If yours is that rare group of individuals who can see all aspects of a project from other than personal angles and make decisions with a minimum of argument, then I congratulate you. Your group will be well-suited to produce. It is possible for all the members of a group to act as co-producers for their recordings, but I have found that this often leads to problems. When two members think a particular guitar solo is great and the other two members think it stinks and has to be redone, who makes the final decision? In situations such as these, the need for a producer becomes clear.

Even with all I have said about the role of the producer as decision maker, the position is not one of dictatorship. The best producers are able to take into account the vision of the artists, the limitations of studio equipment and budget, the realities of the marketplace, the desires of financial backers, and their own experience and ears. While doing all this, they try to keep everyone as happy as possible. Quite a job.

By now I'm sure you are wondering how to make a decision on who should be designated as producer for your project based on the experience and personalities of the people available to you. Let's take a look at the qualities that a good producer should have.

WHAT MAKES A GOOD PRODUCER?

There could be endless arguments among artists, engineers, and record companies about the attributes that the best producers should have. The choice of producer for a particular artist or group is a very personal one. The person who works perfectly with one artist may be awful as an influence with another. This being the case, one thing must be true of your relationship with your producer: You must be able to trust them.

The best producers are half recording engineer, half musician, and half psychiatrist. Hold it! Three halves? Well, some things in life don't add up.

The half of a producer that is a recording engineer gives them the ability to truly understand the many ways a sound can be recorded and enhanced by studio equipment. The engineer in a producer keeps the session from running into technical walls that cannot easily be broached. Creativity is a wonderful thing, but unbridled, too many ideas thrown into a piece can overload your project much like two pounds of baloney in a one pound bag. Even though you may have two pounds of ideas, the recording equipment you are using may not be able to easily process more than one pound. Your music may not need all two pounds of ideas to be compelling. The producer should be able to balance the artistic vision with the equipment used and the budget available.

The audio engineering understanding and background that a producer possesses will allow them to communicate effectively with the session engineer and other studio staffers. The producer's experience with recording studios will also allow them to plan and help execute the technical side of the process in the most efficient manner. If a producer is included early enough in the planning of a project, they will be able to offer valuable advice on the type of studio needed for your project. With good advice, you will not find your project in a studio that is more complex and expensive than necessary or one that is too small and not sophisticated enough.

The half of a producer that is a musician will be able to give an unbiased view of what is being played by the musicians. This doesn't mean whether the musical parts are reflective of the technical facility or creative genius of the player, but rather that the notes are appropriate to the feeling of the piece. This does not include the Emperor of Austria telling Mozart that his piece had "too many notes." That situation was ridiculous because of the difference in musical skills between the two. Many of the best producers are highly skilled and experienced musicians. Their comments and ideas, therefore, engender respect among other musicians. I believe it is impossible for a producer to be really effective if they do not have a thorough understanding of how music works. Most musicians wouldn't trust the opinions of someone who is not a practitioner in the field.

The psychiatrist half of the producer helps the technical side of recording (the engineer and studio staff) communicate with the artistic side (the musicians) without blood being drawn. There are an almost uncountable number of artists who cannot express what they want in a way that an engineer can understand and implement. That's OK. It is not necessarily an artist's job to be able to talk to an engineer in tech-speak. It is the job of the producer to be able to understand both the artist and the engineer. It is also the job of the producer to understand the needs and wants of those who may not be present in the studio but whose happiness may have a great effect on the artist and the product. This includes financial backers, record company personnel, personal managers, and others interested in the outcome of the session. The producer can provide a very necessary buffer between distracting forces and those directly involved in making a recording.

The recording circumstances of unsigned versus signed artists can be quite different. If you are signed to a recording contract, you will, in all like-lihood, find that the record company wants a say in who will produce the recording, especially if they are putting up all or some of the money to record. If you are unsigned or independently financed, your choices are com-pletely open. This does not mean that when choosing a producer the same criteria do not apply. Even though I cannot predict who will be the best pro-ducer for your session, I can go through some of the people you may find yourself considering.

Yourself. At the beginning of their careers, many artists find themselves in the position of having to produce their recordings. The main reason for this is money. Most unsigned artists find themselves with precious little cash to waste on the "luxury" of hiring an experienced independent producer. Even if you have the necessary money, it may be very difficult to interest a "name" pro-ducer in becoming involved with a new, untested artist. This means that your choices can be narrowed to less than world-famous producing help, which would include yourself.

I hope by this time you realize that someone must be firmly ensconced in the producer's chair. If you decide to take on this role yourself, you would do well to treat your choice as if you were considering a stranger. Don't just assume that because you obviously understand the depth and scope of your inspiration that you are necessarily the person to guide the participants and chart the course of your session. Judge your own competence by the same guidelines that you would judge a stranger. You must be honest with yourself on one central question: Do you know enough about how ideas are translated into good recordings? Before deciding on yourself as sole producer, you must ask yourself if you believe that you have at least a majority of the qualities men-tioned above. The reason I say "sole" producer is because many artists have a good perspective on their material but lack experience with recording equip-ment. This lack of experience in recording studios does not eliminate the neo-phyte from inclusion in production decisions. This only means that you may do well producing as part of a team. For many budding producers, this is where the session engineer comes in.

The session engineer. Many unsigned artists end up with the session engineer acting as producer by default. This happens for two reasons. The first is that the engineer is already there, is being paid, and probably has much more practical knowledge of the recording equipment than the artist. The second is that engineers love to produce (like motion picture camera operators who want to direct), and virtually all think that they are capable of producing your project. Even though an engineer may have much more experience at recording then the artists, the real question is do they appreciate the goals and vision of the artist? If you are considering using your engineer as sole producer, then they must be as involved as a producer would be. They must, at least, take enough interest in your project to listen to rehearsal tapes and talk with you about the overall sound and feel you want your recording to have. It would be a very good idea for you to ask if you can listen to other recordings the engineer has produced to see if you like their style. You must trust their instincts with music as well as their ability with machines.

One of the best ways to involve an engineer as producer is to have that person work as co-producer with the artist. In this way, it is possible to have technical wizardry and artistic sensitivity work together hand in hand. This is, of course, assuming that the two people are willing to listen to each other. The artist can guide the creative direction of the project, and the engineer can advise on whether the ideas are practical for the studio being used. This may sound awfully close to the job that you would expect of an engineer who was not co-producing, but if your engineer is aware that they are a co-producer, they will be far more likely to offer creative advice far beyond just twisting knobs. Many engineers will not butt into the creative side of a session for fear of becoming involved in an area where they may not be wanted. If you are expecting advice from your engineer as co-producer, discuss the matter fully. Do not expect that level of involvement if you do not ask for it.

One of your peers. Another artist, whom you know and respect, might be a good choice for producer. This person will surely give the proper weight to artistic matters and might have a perspective on your material that will supply fresh energy and ideas. The best choice among your artistic peers would be someone who understands the type of recording you want to make and has more experience in recording studios than you. Many artists may be willing to help produce a project for another artist for little or no money. A definite plus.

Big-time independent. An independent producer is a person whose specialty is helping artists realize their dreams in recording studios. Some independent producers are stars in their own right and command very high fees, in some cases even getting a percentage of sales revenue from released recordings. Most artists embarking on their first recording projects will not be dealing with high powered producers who are music industry stars or star makers, but they do exist and must be considered. If you can get a well-known producer involved with your project, this alone will greatly increase the chances of getting your music heard or even getting you signed by a record company. Just having the name of a well-known producer on your product will make people take notice. Especially people in the music business.

How can you get a big-time producer interested? The same way you might get anyone involved with your project. Find them, talk to them, play them existing recordings, invite them to a performance, find out what they need to become involved. Even the most well-known producers are always on the lookout for new, exciting talent. The problem is getting them to notice you. Let's say that the sound of the last best-selling album by Bingo and the Honkers completely blew you away, and you would love for your recording to sound like that. You know that your music is just as outrageously cool as Bingo's and so you think, "Hey, their producer might like our sound." So they might. The producer's name is always listed in the credits on an album. Now you have to find out where to get in touch with that person. A good place to start would be the company that released the recording. The name and location of record companies is always listed on their releases. You may have to call information in the city where they are located to get the number of their offices. Through the offices of the release company, you should be able to get contact information of some kind, either an address or phone number, for the producer. It may take a few calls, but be persistent. If the record company cannot or will not give you a contact point, it is always possible to look up the producer's name in industry reference guides (see RESOURCES chapter, "Further Reading"). Never assume that unsolicited submissions will be accepted. Always call first and get an invitation to submit or your stuff may be sent back unopened.

Let's say Bingo's producer thinks that your music is great and agrees to produce your demo or independent album. Have a party. This is a very good thing. Even if this person says they want total control over what will be recorded, this is a very good thing. Even if after you meet this person you think they are a schmuck, this is a very good thing. Even if this person, in your opinion, screws up your recording, this is still a very good thing. Huh? How can this be good? What happened to all the trust and love and stuff I've been describing in good artist-producer relationships? (The author puts on his long gray beard and leans back in a high-backed chair by the fire.) The world being what it is, an association with a well-known professional in the music business may be more valuable in the long run than a lovey-dovey relationship or even a good recording. Hopefully, Mr./Ms. Famous Producer Person is charming, a true professional, and makes you sound like the gods you know you are. Great. You can now pass Go, collect your mega star recording contract, and marry a supermodel (male or female, your choice). What if Bingo's producer acts like an ass and screws up your magnum opus? At least you have a recording you can say they produced. This will go a long way in opening other doors in the music industry and even in getting you a shot at having someone else bankroll another recording.

I'm not saying that an artist necessarily needs to put up with a producer who is really difficult to work with. I am also not saying that well-known people in the music business are necessarily buttheads. The point here is that if you, a person with relatively little influence in the music industry, hook up with a person who has a large amount of influence, it is better for you to work with them than not. Whatever the outcome, you will have a foot in the door. (Remove beard.)

Not so big-time independent. There are many people who are qualified independent producers who are not working and hanging out with the jet set in Monte Carlo. These may include people in your area who have produced recordings for other local artists. How do you find them? You would do well to locate other artists and find out if they will recommend their producers. Even if the material on other artists' recordings is stylistically quite different from what you want to record, don't necessarily count their producer out. If the other artist worked well with them and a good-sounding recording resulted, you should at least talk to the producer, listen to other projects they have worked on, and hear what they have to say about yours. Chances are, they have worked on many different types of recordings and may be in a position to do a good job for you. The recording studios you will talk to when deciding which to use will have the names of independent producers. Ask the various studios you are considering if they can recommend any.

If an independent producer has any contacts with record companies or other music industry professionals you might want to get your finished product to, so much the better. If a producer has worked with acts that were subsequently signed to recording contracts, they may be able to help you with getting your music heard at those labels. Take attitude, experience, contacts, and price all into consideration.

Staff producers. Most artists who are not signed to record contracts will not be faced with the prospect of using a staff producer. In the old days, record companies built and operated their own studios and had producers on staff. Virtually all artists signed to a label used the label's own studios and producers. As the use of independent studios blossomed, so did the numbers and influence of independent producers. Even though most recordings today are made in independent studios, even for the biggest labels, record companies still have producers on staff. Staff producers work for record companies either on retainer or on a project-by-project basis. The biggest difference between them and pure independents is that they are chosen and paid by the record companies who back artists. This is one way that the people spending the money for a recording retain a measure of control over what happens in the studio. At smaller labels, the owner of the label may insist on producing all of the recordings their artists make for them. In almost all cases, record companies, regardless of size, will want to have a say in who is going to produce a recording for one of their artists.

The record company is dependent on the producer to help the artist come up with a product that is successful not only creatively but also commercially. The staff producer, therefore, has two viewpoints to consider: the artist's and the company's. The artists want creative integrity at all costs, and the label wants a hit at all costs. The producer tries to satisfy both parties. Not ever an easy job.

Some record contracts give the company complete power to pick a producer. In some rare cases, new artists are allowed total freedom to choose their own producer. It is likely that your situation will fall somewhere in between. Your label may suggest some names to you, and they might ask if you have anyone in mind. If you are signed to a record company that wants a say in who produces your recording, this is not necessarily a bad thing. It is highly probable that the producers that work for your label are experienced, sensitive professionals who will do their best to make you sound your best. Give them the benefit of the doubt and treat all suggestions from your label seriously. Apply the same criteria that you would when considering an independent, but take into account the fact that this is someone your label already likes. There are probably very good reasons for this. If you are going to submit a name to your label as a possible producer, make sure you have solid reasons for your choice. Just because you think they are really cool usually isn't good enough. Suggest someone for whom you can make an argument in the areas of attitude, experience, and price. This will help you get your suggestion taken seriously.

In conclusion, it can generally be said that an independent producer will have the artist's happiness at the top of their list, and a staff producer, paid by a record company, is obviously working for that company at least as much as for the artist. Understanding this will help you make an educated choice and will also help you appreciate the role of the person producing your recording.

Chapter 3

The Engineer

The sorcerer wears a tall, pointed hat covered with images of transistors and digital logic probes. The wizard's hands move with blinding speed over the mysterious and terrifying sliders, knobs, and flashing lights that are implanted in the witch's familiar, known to those possessed by the spirits of the black arts as "The Recording Console." The small group of lowly musicians trembles as the magician turns to regard them with cold, flashing, steel-blue eyes and utters the terrible question: "So, ready for playback?"

All right, maybe you're not going to be recording in Merlin's lair, but many people still have the notion that a recording engineer is some sort of witch doctor with special powers. Special powers maybe, because the engineer probably knows a lot more than you about running the equipment in a recording studio. Aside from that, what do they do and how should they do it? This chapter will demystify the role and qualities of a good recording engineer. Read on, Grasshopper.

THE ENGINEER'S ROLE

The most obvious part of a recording engineer's duties is to run the equipment in a recording studio. Even though the main benefit an engineer should bring to your session is familiarity with recording equipment, there are many ways an engineer can help or hurt your session. Recording engineers are part of the filter through which your ideas must pass before they emerge on tape.

Example of a Track Sheet

XYZ Studios	CLIENT:			PO#	SPEED:	ENGINEER:		REEL NO:
ARTIST:	PRODUCER:			DATE:	STUDIO:	NOISE REDUCTION:		
SELECTION 1	1	2	3	4	5	6	7	8
	9	10	11	12	13	14	15	16
	17	18	19	20	21	22	23	24
SELECTION 2	1	2	3	4	5	6	7	8
	9	10	11	12	13	14	15	16
	17	18	19	20	21	22	23	24
SELECTION 3	1	2	3	4	5	6	7	8
	9	10	11	12	13	14	15	16
	17	18	19	20	21	22	23	24
COMMENTS:								

A good engineer helps with that process all along the way, not just when tape is rolling.

The recording engineer is in charge of all of the equipment in the studio. To a large extent, this means your personal equipment as well. The engineer will decide, with the input of the producer, which pieces of equipment will work the best to transcribe your sound onto tape. This includes type and placement of microphones, placement of musicians, settings on musicians' personal equipment, as well as connections and settings of all studio equipment. Just because you may have spent years learning how to get the perfect sound out of your instruments and amps in performance doesn't mean that an engineer is trying to mess up your sound if they ask you to change some settings or playing techniques. Microphones and recording gear do not react to sound in the same way as the human ear, and sometimes it may be necessary for artists to make adjustments to get the right sound on tape.

The engineer is also in charge of the secretarial work generated by a session, unless an assistant is given these tasks. This doesn't mean typing a letter to your manager. During the course of your session, track sheets should be kept to identify what is recorded on each of the recorder's many tracks for each song (see page 35). For example: Track 1, bass guitar; Track 2, snare drum; Track 3, bass drum; and so on. This is usually done on blank forms that the studio has made to match the configuration of their equipment. The track sheets should also contain a variety of technical information about the settings of the recorder used for that session. This eliminates confusion in the future when the multitrack tape is pulled back out of its box and slapped on another recorder. The engineer also needs to make sure that a particular reel or cartridge of multitrack tape, its box, and the appropriate track sheet are all marked so as to be easily matched up.

Take sheets should also be kept during the course of the session (see page 37). A "take" is the term used for a recorded version of a song. Even a false start, if not recorded over, should be given a take number. A take sheet will also be kept on a blank form that the studio has and should include take number, tape position counter reading, length of the take in real time, title of the piece, and comments on the take. Comments could include "false start," "good solo, ending weak," "good," etc. These comments make it easy to identify and roll right up to the desired take later on. Take sheets should also be marked to be easily mated with the proper tape.

Some studios also keep board sheets on which the recording console's various control settings can be marked for recall at a later time. The settings of effects devices may also be noted. If automated or computer-controlled equipment is used, it is the engineer's responsibility to make sure that all relevant information is saved. If this generates computer disks or tapes that you will keep, they too must be properly marked. Just this housekeeping alone would make your engineer a pretty busy person.

The engineer should also be available for technical advice as to how best to achieve what the producer and artist want. Part of the engineer's role is to answer questions that the artist or producer might have about the operation and capabilities of the studio equipment. Even though the engineer is there to supply answers, don't let your session turn into a class on recording. This will slow down the process and distract the engineer. If you want to learn about recording in that studio, set a later date.

Speaking of learning about recording, many musicians own home recording equipment these days which allows them to multitrack. This is great not only for the creative outlets that this technology gives to artists, but because it allows musicians to learn something about the process of multitrack

Example of a Take Sheet

XYZ Studios			ARTIST:	DATE:	REEL NO:
TAKE NO	CNTR NO	TIME	TITLE		COMMENTS
1	0:00				*False start.*
2	0:20	3:30			*Good solo, ending weak.*
3	3:50	3:29			*Good.*
4					
5					
6					
7					
8					
9					
10					
11					
12					
13					
14					
15					

recording. This is a very good thing for the musicians but can be not so good for engineers. I have witnessed scenes in studios where artists wanted to argue with the engineer's methods because they were not used to recording that way on their home machines. Make no mistake, the equipment in a recording studio is not a slightly larger version of what many people have at home. Almost everything about the settings, capabilities, and response of studio equipment will be different from your average 4-track cassette recorder.

If you have experience with home multitrack equipment and have techniques or settings that you find usually work well to get your sound, mentioning these things is always appropriate. Insisting on a certain procedure or setting that the engineer says will not sit well with the studio equipment will only be counterproductive. If you have some experience with your home recorder, use it to your and your engineer's advantage. Mention things that work for you at home—an engineer should always be ready to listen to this—then be open to the fact that things will not be exactly the same in a recording studio.

The engineer's familiarity with the particular equipment in his studio will also be invaluable to the producer of your session in session planning and in post-session processes. If your producer can have an in-depth discussion with the engineer about what you expect to achieve during your session, they can develop a road map for the process and save a lot of time during the session.

Once recording has commenced, the engineer watches all the level indicators to ensure that no overloading is taking place. Levels may have to be adjusted through the faders on the recording console while recording is taking place. Both the producer and the engineer may be involved. The engineer also helps the producer by being a second set of ears. The engineer may notice a mistake or missed note that the producer does not. An engineer should always point out possible problems with the performance, but this opinion is always subservient to the opinions of the producer and artist.

During the mix, it is the responsibility of the engineer to manipulate the relative volume and tonal balances of the tracks. It is also the engineer's job to listen to the mix to detect possible technical problems, buzzes, rattles, squeaks, sneezes, etc. It is quite acceptable for the engineer to make suggestions on tonal quality, use of effects, and other parameters of the recording during tracking and mixdown. Acting on a suggestion is always at the discretion of the producer or artists.

WHAT MAKES A GOOD ENGINEER?

The qualities of a good engineer are less nebulous then those of a good producer. No matter what qualifications an engineer may have, one quality overrides all others: The engineer should always try to be cooperative. The phrases I hate to hear from engineers are, "I won't," "I never," or "I don't do that." To be sure, there are some things that recording equipment just is not designed to do, but I have found that most requests by clients are not so outlandish that they should not even be attempted. What good is the world's most skilled engineer if they won't cooperate? Unfortunately, I have run into uncooperative engineers too often not to mention the possibility that you may also. I am an engineer myself and own my own recording service. I am not out to bash engineers. Most professional recording engineers are ready and willing to do whatever is necessary to help a session along.

Occasionally, one runs into a knob-twister who, for whatever reason, tries to dissuade artists from trying something unfamiliar to the engineer. To those not experienced in recording studios, this may cause tension and confusion. After all, the engineer is supposed to know what they are doing and the request does not seem to be out of line. If an engineer objects to a procedure that the artist or producer wants to try, then there should be a specific and understandable technical reason for the objection. "We don't do it that way here," is never acceptable. A large part of the engineer's job is to help you feel comfortable with what you are doing, assuming that what you are doing will work for your recording. After cooperation, technical knowledge, experience, and familiarity with the equipment in the studio you are going to use are at the top of the list.

You will probably first come into contact, professionally, with recording engineers during the phase of your session when you are auditioning studios. An engineer will most likely be the person to show you around the studio and explain all of its fabulous and unique features. These first meetings are actually a very good place to start sizing up the person you might be using as engineer for your session. While large multimillion dollar recording plants may have a dozen or more engineers on staff, most small to medium-sized studios have one or two people who are the "in-house" engineers. Most hourly rates for studios include the services of an in-house engineer. This being the case, the person you meet may be the same person who will engineer your session. It is a very good idea to ask if the person who gives you the tour is the sole house engineer or if there are others on staff. If there are, get their names; you will want to talk to them later.

If more than one person is on the engineering staff of a studio, you should do your best to talk to them all. You may not feel that you want your tour guide to work your session, but there may be another staff member who is just your cup of tea. A lot will depend on how comfortable you are with the personality of your engineer. There may be senior and junior engineers on the staff of the studio who command different rates. Never assume that all the members of a staff will be available at the same rate.

There is quite a bit to be said in favor of using the person who is most experienced with the unique configuration of a particular studio. There is no such thing as a generic recording studio. They are all different and have their own special qualities. The staff engineers who are used to working in their studio day in and day out are intimate with the peculiarities of that studio's equipment and rooms. Staff engineers will usually be the people who understand how to best use these features quickly and efficiently to your benefit.

This does not mean that there is no room in the world for the independent recording engineer. Far from it. There are situations where an independent engineer will be better for your session then a staffer. Let's say that there is a beautiful 32-track digital recording studio right in your town where you can buy time for a special low rate. The only problem is that they specialize in recording country music and you do not feel comfortable using their engineer to lay down screaming tracks for your alternative rock band. This is where the independent comes in. Independent engineers can be found in much the same way as independent producers. An independent engineer experienced in the techniques used to get the sounds necessary for your type of music could be found and brought in for your session. Don't expect that the studio will not want one of their staffers to be present during sessions. Most studios will and may still expect you to pay for their presence, perhaps at a reduced rate. A good independent engineer should appreciate having a person there who is intimate with the studio.

Any good engineer should be the possessor of a large bag of tricks. This means they know many different ways of getting good sound onto tape. Just as no two artists sound exactly alike, no one technique is good for recording all sounds. Good engineers are constantly updating and adding to their bag of tricks and are willing and even excited to drag any of them out.

Some engineers are known for their expertise with particular phases of the recording process. It is quite common to find one engineer credited with the recording of a commercial release, another named as mix engineer, and a third as mastering engineer. All areas of recording have their specialists. Most artists just beginning their recording careers will not have the budget to hire famous specialists for their session. You should ask if an engineer you are considering using was involved in all parts of a recording that was played for you as an example of their work.

Even if you do not have all the money in the world, you can still consider, and may be able to afford, the help of a specialist. You may only need them for a few hours. Most specialist engineers are brought in during mix sessions. For example, it may be well worth the extra money to get the assistance of an engineer who has tons of experience and a good reputation for working on dancehall reggae mixes if that is what you are recording. Many types of music have mix or recording techniques that are particular to that style. A specialist may get you closer to your dream in less time.

An engineer who seems genuinely stimulated at the prospect of recording your session is someone who has one important quality you want: interest. No session should be treated by an engineer as the same old thing. No matter how many times they may have done this and no matter how small your project, the engineer should be doing everything to make the result as good as possible.

The best engineers will be cooperative, knowledgeable, efficient, and interested.

Chapter 4

Choosing
a Studio

So you've chosen your songs, rehearsed until your neighbors called the cops, had your amps and instruments tweaked, refined your attitude, have your deal or budget in hand, and perhaps secured the services of an independent producer or engineer; now it's time to enter the belly of the beast and choose a studio. "Well, the cheapest ought to do." "I want the biggest place we can afford." "Let's get the joint that Skunk & the Pumpkins used for their last album." "My friend's got a tape recorder." All valid reasons to consider a studio as a possibility but dangerous if used as the only criteria. Unless you have fairly extensive experience with, and have been satisfied with, the results from a particular facility, you should undertake a search process.

The recording studio is the place where your ideas can be spun into potential gold or where your hit can hit the fan. A poorly considered decision on a studio can sow the seeds for trouble. Aside from the artist's preparation, getting your project into the right facility is the single most important step towards a final product that meets your expectations. Transferring ideas onto tape, whether single sounds or multiple instruments and voices, is almost never a simple matter. The process of producing a successful recording is one that combines the best equipment you can afford with the best people you can find. The combination of the two will provide you with your best chance of success.

Recording studios are much more than just a pile of expensive, mysterious equipment with lots of pretty lights. The people involved can make or break your project. Professionalism and flexibility are key attributes in both equipment and personnel. Professionalism on the part of personnel is not necessarily defined by how many hit recordings that person may be associated with but by their willingness and ability to do what is necessary to benefit your project. The best professional equipment is not necessarily the most expensive; more important is whether or not it will produce the desired effect. If your studio staff is flexible, they will approach your project without preconceptions of what will work for you. If you have found that you can get that perfect sound and feel for your sax solo only while playing in a bathroom standing on a toilet, and the studio has a suitable bathroom, they ought to at least try to record you in there. There may be things that are impossible for technical or practical reasons in particular studios (there just isn't a way to get the elephant into the building), but one should never have to accept the "we don't do it that way" school of thought. Studio staff should at least be willing to consider all possibilities and explain why they may or may not work. I have heard and been involved in too many sessions that were ruined by the wrong combination of people even though they were using the most sophisticated equipment in the world.

Now don't get me wrong—modern, properly maintained recording gear is a very important part of producing master quality products, but I am assuming that you do not have the budget of Top Ten acts and are trying to do the best you can with more limited means. If you are not an audio engineer yourself, how do you make a decision between the many different types of setups you are likely to come across in your search for the perfect rig? A great place to start is to solicit recommendations and opinions from other musicians in your area. If you can, ask to listen to their final product. If the artist can't or won't get you a copy, the studio where the tape was made ought to be willing to let you hear examples if you make an appointment and let them know you are thinking of using them for a project. Be sure to find out who engineered and mixed the tracks and if there was any major equipment brought in from outside. It would be quite a disappointment to find out that the crystal clear sound you heard on the other band's tape was achieved with the use of a rented recorder that is no longer in the studio.

Studios sell and change their gear on a regular basis. If you are considering a facility because they have specific pieces of equipment or instruments on hand, make sure those items will be available for your session. I worked in a studio in NY that had all of the wonderful percussion instruments of a symphony orchestra in the main recording room. If I were considering using a studio because of a rare find in terms of on-hand equipment like that, I would want to guarantee that the stuff would be there for my session. Just because you see something in the room doesn't automatically mean it will be there for you. They might be thinking of selling the whole lot in two weeks!

Style is also an important factor in choosing a studio. No, I'm not talking about what type of potted plants they have or the color of the carpet. I'm talking about experience with your musical style. I was once forced to waste hours struggling to get a NY studio to understand how to record a cranked-up-loud Marshall guitar amplifier because, although this was a professional multitrack facility, they were used almost exclusively for voice-over recording, commercials, and classical music! Who booked that session?

I did. It was many years ago, deep in the mists of time, when this Grasshopper was not learned in many of the sacred ways of the recording temples. I learned a valuable lesson. Don't book studio time based on price and equipment alone. If the studio you are considering does not have at least some experience with, or understanding of, the type of music you will be recording, chances are you are starting on an uphill climb.

If you have secured the services of an independent engineer or producer you can trust (why use them if you can't trust them?), they should be actively involved in the studio selection process, and I would defer to their judgment. They probably understand the equipment and the whole process of getting a session to successful completion better than you and hopefully have had experience with, and know the capabilities of, studios that could handle your project. Unless you are willing to pay them for their time, don't expect an independent producer or engineer to undertake the entire process of an extended search. Should you wish to consider facilities other than those recommended by your producer or independent engineer, get as much information from those studios as you can through your own inquiries. Pass the info along and ask if these other studios should be considered. If a situation recommended by someone else makes you really nervous, like a producer insisting on a facility that your band really can't afford, it's probably time to question your reasons for working with that person.

Let's say you are on your own, as are many acts who are starting out. How do you make a choice? Let's run down the categories.

LOCATION

A great studio that you can afford right around the corner is ideal...and, sadly, almost never a reality. I would start out by calling all the places in your town and asking them to send you their information and rate card. This may be a beautiful color brochure or a hand-typed letter. In any event, it should give you a general idea of what type of projects they can handle and a solid price quote of dollars per hour. You can start your selection process right there. If you have a $500 budget and are quoted a rate of $350 per hour, chances are you can't afford that particular situation.

If you live in a small town, this process may start and end on the same day. If you live in NY, LA, or other large urban areas, this could take quite a lot of phone calls. Take my word for it, contact as many as you can; it's worth it. You never know who is out there waiting to give you a great deal on just the type of facility you need. If your town doesn't offer many choices, I would expand your search area. It would certainly be worth the time, trouble, and even the extra money to travel a few hundred miles to end up with a really great tape.

If you are considering an out-of-town facility, get as much information as you can. Describe, in as much detail as possible, what you would like to record, how you might like it done, and what type of final product you envision (e.g., demo cassette, CD, video soundtrack).

Get a detailed description of the physical aspects of the studio. Is it large enough for your needs? Is it too big? Some voice-over studios are little more than closets with a microphone. Other studios may be ridiculously large and, therefore, a waste of money for a solo act. If you can find a studio closely tailored to your needs, you will get maximum bang for your buck.

If at all possible, I strongly recommend that you make every effort to visit any facility you are seriously considering. This is easy with in-town locations but also makes a lot of sense with out-of-town locations. The place that looks and sounds so good from their brochure and descriptions may have turned into a wreck in the past few years. Go and look.

After you have considered as many options as you can, try and narrow your choices down to the closest facilities that you think you can afford. But how do you know what you can afford?

RATES

Don't be put off by what seems to be a high rate card figure. This is usually the rate a studio charges corporate clients for prime time. Discounts for all types of reasons, block booking several hours, recording in off hours, or just because they like you, are usually available and can be quite substantial. Of course, if a rate card quotes $350 per hour for recording time, it is unlikely that a discount to $25 per hour will be forthcoming; but, hey, it's worth a shot. I have been in some top-flight studios in NY that discounted as much as 85 percent because of a combination of reasons. There are almost no studios that are booked 24 hours a day, and they are all looking to fill up that dead time somehow. Even at very expensive facilities, some money is better than no money. So don't rule out any place just because of rates until you propose a deal.

What type of a deal is a deal? They can take almost any form. I have known of studios that, while in the process of expanding, traded recording time for help with carpentry. I have personally been able to trade big discounts on rates for playing at the studio's private parties. Maybe you are in another business that can be helpful to the owners. Use your imagination and find out. Some places insist on cash only but many do not. I know that if the owners of the local service station wanted to trade auto repairs for recording time in my studio, I would go for it. I love my 1972 Chevy, but it requires lots of tender loving care.

Some studios will entertain the idea of a "spec" deal (for further explanation of spec deals, see APPENDIX). Find out. Figure out all your assets and options and try to use them.

Some studios will insist on a deposit to hold time open. Some will expect several payments if your project is going to take a while. Most will not release a finished master tape until final payment is made. Make sure that you and the studio personnel are clear about how and when payment will be tendered. A simple letter of agreement outlining the terms should be sufficient. The studio should be willing to draw up two copies of this document so both parties can sign and have a copy.

Remember, you are paying for both the time of the people running the studio and the equipment that will be used in your session. We've already discussed the people involved (engineer, producer, etc.) in Chapters 2 and 3, but how do you decide what equipment is right for your project?

STUDIO EQUIPMENT

Without getting into the details of technology, which is not the purpose of this book, there are still some basic questions that you, the expectant recordist, must ask.

What types of musical instruments and equipment does the studio own, and is their use included in the hourly rate? If you are a jazz pianist, you obviously need a room with a professional-grade piano. If your band does not own the best amplifiers or drums, does the studio have better ones?

The more complicated your project, the more you will probably need in the way of tracks on a multitrack tape recorder, input channels on the mixing board, pieces of special electronics effects, processing gear, and high-quality microphones. Even if you know precious little about the specialized equipment used in modern studios, you still need to use your head. If you have a seventeen-piece funk band with a five-piece horn section and backup singers, you will probably need a studio with a large number of quality microphones. I've used as many as twelve to mike a drum set alone! If you are a solo singer and guitarist, you might be able to get away with one really good microphone.

Never assume that everything you see in a studio recording or control room is included in the basic hourly rate. Some places charge an extra fee for the use of specialized or very expensive equipment. If you want to use something, ask if it's included.

Many people overlook recording tape in figuring the overall cost of their project. Unless you are going to record to computer hard disk or a wax cylinder, professional-grade recording tape can eat up a large part of your budget. Most professional recording machines use types of tape not normally available in your local Radio Shack. Some of these tape formats can exceed $200 for twenty minutes' worth of tape. Ouch! Most studios will charge a premium, some more than others, for obtaining the necessary tape. After all, they are providing a service. All studios will be able to sell you the particular tape formats that they use, but they are not the only source and they should not insist that you buy your tape from them. As long as you get the right brand and type of tape, a studio should be willing to use blank tape that you provide. Ask them specifically what brand and types they prefer to use. (For more on recording tape and costs, see Chapter 1, "Budgeting Your Project.")

If you live in a large city, there are probably places in town where you can buy the types of tape the studio specifies. Look in the Audio-Visual Suppliers section in your local yellow pages and do some searching. If no suppliers are available in your area, investigate mail-order sources advertising in magazines such as *Electronic Musician, Guitar Player,* etc. You may be able to find what you need at a discount.

Many studios will have used tape that they can effectively erase and sell to you for as little as half the price of virgin tape. Even though virgin tape is ideal, most professional recording tape can be used more than once without a great loss of fidelity. It is well known in the industry that the band Heart recorded their first commercial release, *Dreamboat Annie,* which went on to sell millions of copies, on used tape. Ask about the availability of used tape if you are concerned about the cost of new. Every dollar you save on things like tape can be put into more recording or mixing time, and everybody needs more of that.

In all cases, try and describe to the studio personnel what you expect to record and what the finished product should sound like. I have found that most studios will be honest about whether they can handle your project, and if so how, assuming they understand what you want.

BOOKING TIME

"Time and tide wait for no man." This phrase holds true for all in recording studios. What you are really buying when you hand over your hard-earned bucks is time. Time to play with all that nifty stuff they have, the engineer's time, the producer's time, the time needed to keep the recording equipment in good repair, and on and on. The goal of the artist is to maximize the time that is purchased in the studio. None but the most well-heeled of musicians can afford to spend time, and money, in a recording studio without making progress towards the finished product. It may be just fine for acts who are signed to major labels and have several platinum albums under their belts to spend a month in a world-class recording studio in Switzerland, writing songs and rehearsing for their new album. But most of the readers of this book will not have that kind of budget. The amount of time necessary to record and mix a selection depends on the artists involved, the type and complexity of the instrumentation, and the expectations surrounding the finished product. A demo session might take much less time than polishing a recording for release on CD.

Virtually all recording sessions can be broken up into three sections: setting up, recording, and mixing. None of these categories can be ignored or shortchanged when booking studio time. If you do, you will find yourself running over time and over budget. Each time an artist or band enters a studio to perform or mix is considered a separate session. Even though you might not get a full mix by the end of each session, you will almost always want to run off a few cassettes, so that the producer and artist will be able to listen to and reflect on what was accomplished.

For any session, large or small, set-up time is necessary. If your session begins at noon, don't expect to walk in and begin at 12:00 on the dot. Even for the simplest of sessions, a solo instrument let's say, the studio personnel will have to set up and plug in microphones, set levels and tones on the mixing board, load tape into the recorder, patch in and set parameters for effects and outboard devices, and finally, record a small section to play back to you or the producer to see if the settings are satisfactory. As you can see, this could easily take thirty minutes to an hour even with the swiftest studio rats scurrying around. Do not try to rush your set ups. This usually results in either having to do it all over again later or producing generally unsatisfactory results. Make sure to allow adequate set-up time for each session along the way of your project. Some set-up time can be saved if you can schedule back-to-back sessions. For example, session #1 from 8 p.m. to 1 a.m.; session #2, the next day, from 10 a.m. to 2 p.m. You could leave your equipment overnight and return the next day to resume recording without having to set up all over again. This type of scheduling, of course, assumes that no sessions are booked in the room during the down time between sessions.

The studio personnel and your producer will be able to give a good estimate of how much set-up time will be needed, if they have an accurate picture of what is going to happen. "Hi, I just happened to meet this six-piece horn section in the bar across the street, and I'd like to throw them in." That's just fine, but it will blow your estimate of set-up time. Staying within that estimate can be very important. Most sessions are not open ended; they have a definite cutoff time. I've found that people also have a definite cutoff time, even if you have all the studio time in the world. Extra time spent setting up will probably have to come at the expense of recording or mixing time and will certainly bore the other musicians who were not expecting to wait that long. If you want to add that horn section, get their phone numbers and do it at a later date.

The time necessary to play and record the material is always many multiples of the time of the actual piece. Say you've got a five-piece band and you want to record two songs of five minutes each. You might think that a little more than ten minutes would be sufficient to do the actual recording. This is almost never the case. Time will be eaten up by false starts, by someone playing louder or softer than they did during set up, by dropped guitar picks, and (I know this never happens to you) by flat-out mistakes. Even when a good take is laid down, the producer and artist will want to listen to what was just played to make sure that everything was recorded well. And second or third versions are almost always recorded to have several choices. Add discussion time, coffee drinking, fiddling with amps and instruments, and a little fooling around, and it can easily take an hour to get a good take of a five-minute song. This is exclusive of any overdubs that might be necessary.

After completing set up and recording, the producer and artist will almost always want to have rough mixes run off on cassettes, so that the session can be listened to outside of the studio. This will also take some time, and an hour for this purpose is not out of the ordinary. The band can use this time to take down their instruments if necessary.

Our five-piece band, wanting only to record and not go to final mix, could easily use five-and-a-half hours of studio time to record the tracks for two songs of five minutes each. If this is what the studio personnel and the producer think will be necessary, then that is the amount of time that should be booked. Trying to save a few dollars by saying, "Oh, I know we can do it quicker than that," and booking less time will probably turn out to be counterproductive.

Final mix is usually best left to a session all by itself. This can be a complicated and time-consuming process that deserves as much attention as the actual playing does. A final mix session still follows the format of your other sessions: set up, work, and copies/break down. Set-up time is for configuring the control room to the needs of your particular mix, setting levels on the board, and loading tapes. Work time is for performing the mixes themselves. And copies/break-down time is for running off copies of the final mix and "zeroing out" the control room. The amount of time a final mix session will take depends on how much needs to be "fixed in the mix," how complex your piece is, and what your expectations are. Special effects, like tape manipulation for backward guitar solos or lots of sampling, eat up lots of time. Let your producer or studio personnel know about any special ideas you might have and follow their advice so you book enough time.

The last considerations are how many hours to book back to back and when to schedule the sessions. No matter how glad an artist is to be there, a studio can become a claustrophobic environment very quickly. If our fictional five-piece band totals five-and-a-half hours for recording and six hours for final mix, is a single eleven-and-a-half hour session the way to go? In most cases not. Some studios might give you a substantial discount for using hard-to-book time, like Sunday night/Monday morning; and if, under those circumstances, one long session is the only way you can afford to do it, then do it. In most cases, though, it is better to limit the time spent in the studio during one session. What are you like after an eight-hour work day? Ready to go home and open a cold one, I bet. The same holds true for recording sessions. Even if you have the time, if the participants are tired and have heard the same song four hundred times in the last six hours, you can bet they are no longer sharp. Some people have the energy and concentration to work marathon sessions, but this is rare, and I have found that six to eight hours is about the limit for most people. Even if you have musicians coming and going at different times during the session, your producer and engineer are going to be there the whole time.

Going by the guidelines stated, our five-piece ensemble would probably do well to book a six-hour session to record the tracks for their two songs and a separate six-hour session for final mixdown. If you do find yourself getting done early, the studio will probably be willing to subtract the cost of time not used. It might be a good idea to talk about this possibility when first booking time. Obviously, more or less complicated projects require more or less total time. It is usually a good idea to leave at least a day between recording and final mix to give you and your producer a chance to listen to the rough mix at home and make notes: "lots of reverb on guitar solo," "harmony vocals louder in chorus," etc. Written notes can be very important. There will be a lot to remember during the course of overdubbing and mixing, and with a check list, not even the smallest tweak will be forgotten.

Well, by now you have hopefully found a studio that is in your price range, within reach of a jumbo jet, with all the right stuff, just your size, and with the right time slots open. Congrats! Now get ready to pass Go and embark upon the sessions!

Chapter 5

The
Sessions

The sessions are where it's all going to happen. Where your dreams—standing in the center of a darkened recording room, the sound of the brilliant backing tracks pounding in your headphones, while you are struck by divine lightning and deliver the solo track worthy of the gods—will all come true. Or not.

I have seen some brilliant and totally unplanned things happen during recording and mix sessions, but the meat of the matter on most successful recordings is accomplished through planning and good preparation. Preparation for the sessions was covered in the preceding chapters, but now it is time to plan the sessions.

PLANNING YOUR RECORDING SESSIONS

If you and your producer, engineer, and studio staff have had your discussions and booked time well, it is time to plan what is going to happen during that time. Musicians and their equipment will need to arrive in time to set up and be ready to play by the time the actual recording process begins. As I mentioned in the last chapter, some instruments take a lot more time to set up than others.

The more complicated the instrumentation becomes, the more time is needed for set up. The most complicated instruments to set up should be the first to arrive at a session. For most bands, this will be the drummer and their boxes full of things to hit, slap, rattle, bang, thump, and pummel. Drum sets are usually the most complicated part of a band's rig and are also the hardest instrument in most bands to mike and get to shut up.

Get to shut up? We thought the idea was to make noise! Ah, yes, Grasshoppers, but only the noises you want to appear on tape. Most drum sets, and many other instruments, are full of buzzings, wheezings, squeakings, and other unwanted sounds that may not sound terribly nasty on a stage at 4000 decibels but, in front of a highly sensitive studio microphone, sound like dinosaur farts. These take time to silence and silenced they should be! Once committed to tape, a squeaky bass drum pedal can only be fixed by re-recording the track—a process more costly and time consuming than fixing the thing in the first place.

What works well in most cases is to layer the arrival time of the band members according to their set-up needs. If you have a five-piece rock band (drums, bass, guitar, sax, keyboards), your arrival and set-up times might look like this:

Noon — Drums
1:00 — Keyboards
1:30 — Bass and Guitar
2:00 — Sax and Singers
2:30 — Start Recording

As you can see, a full hour has been given to setting up the drum set and its microphones. I have been involved in sessions where it took more than five hours to get the desired sounds on a drum set. A half hour each to the keyboards, bass and guitar, and another half hour to the sax and microphones for vocals. Even if the singers also play instruments, separate mics and levels will need to be set up for their vocal parts. Two-and-a-half hours of set-up time is not unreasonable for this band. The drummer and keyboard player could even be sent out to get lunch for the rest of the band after their instruments are set. They have an hour to an hour-and-a-half of free time before playing begins. They can't practice, because setup must be a fairly quiet time, so give them something useful to do.

Be sure that all persons expected at a session are aware of their arrival and playing times. I always double check with each person involved in a session the day before for two reasons. The first is that any details that may have been forgotten can be taken care of; and the second is that even recent conversations have a way of being mentally misplaced. Make sure that all participants have the phone number of the studio with them on the day of the recording, so an emergency, flat tire, etc., can be dealt with by those already at the studio.

Decide beforehand the order in which songs will be recorded. It is usually a good idea to try the less complicated and less energetic pieces first. This gives the players and singers a chance to warm up and does not blow them out on the first take. Getting good tracks down right off on a slower and perhaps easier-to-play tune also gives those involved a feeling of confidence about the whole undertaking. Confidence and a relaxed feeling go a long way to getting the best possible performances out of the artists.

There are two basic ways to go about recording a song. One is to record all the parts "live," with all the parts, instrumental and vocal, recorded at the same time. This method is rarely used in studio recordings because it is hard to get the best possible tracks from all performers at once. The more common technique is to build a song on tape by recording the rhythm tracks (drums, bass, rhythm guitar) first and then adding or overdubbing other tracks, like lead guitar and vocals. If you are planning a session in which several songs are to be recorded and you are planning to record rhythm track and overdubs at the same session, I find it is better to finish all tracks for a given song before moving on to the next. The players and singers do better when concentrating on one tune at a time, rather than recording the rhythm tracks for all the songs and then going back and laying down the overdubs.

Many times one encounters a disease known as Red Light Fever; this can affect even very experienced players. Red Light Fever causes people to stiffen up and not be relaxed about their playing when the engineer says, "OK, this is going to be a take," and the little red recording light goes on. A trick I learned a long time ago is to tell the band that they are just going to rehearse a tune before recording it, and then go ahead and record this "rehearsal" without telling them. This is not really as mean and tricky as it sounds. The artist's first shot at a song is very often the best version they will play that day. It would be a shame to lose it. If the rehearsal recording does get messed up in some way, that section of tape can always be recorded over with another version. If it turns out well, then your first take is done and you can move on.

STUDIO ETIQUETTE

Finger bowls please, and raise your pinkies! This is not what I mean by studio etiquette. How you and the other members of your session group behave during your session can affect how you are treated by the staff, how seriously they treat your project, and the quality of the final result. There are no special, super secret rules of behavior regarding studios, but there are some gaffes you might not know about and can avoid with a little warning.

Be on time! If you have booked and confirmed a session, the studio personnel will be expecting you at the time specified. If you are a half hour late in arriving, do not expect that time to be added to the end of your session for free. I would suggest planning on arriving at least a half hour early. If the studio is empty before your session, you might get a half hour of set-up time for free. At least you know you will be in the hall, instruments in hand, when your time arrives.

Make sure that you confirm with each member of the session, preferably on the day before, that they know when they are to arrive at the studio and how they are to get there. Get in touch with each session member personally. Don't rely on leaving a message or having one bandmember call another. Somehow this type of arrangement always gets messed up at the worst possible time.

Don't eat lunch on the recording console! Or any other equipment for that matter. Almost all sessions are long enough for the participants to feel the need for a Coke, coffee, or some other refreshment. Longer sessions might even include eating take-out meals. In all cases, ask studio personnel what surfaces would be appropriate for eating a sandwich on or even for putting down a cup of coffee. What looks like a small end table to you could actually be a rack with several thousands of dollars' worth of electronics in it. A studio engineer will definitely take a dim view of having a super-sized drink perched on any surface near an expensive mixing desk, piano, tape recorder, or any other studio-owned equipment. Most studios will be happy to provide or show you which surfaces or areas they consider safe for drinks and eats. I would keep such items off your equipment as well. It may not be any skin off the nose of the studio if you spill a Slurpee into the back of your vintage Marshall amp, but it will sure put a crimp in the style of your session. Play it extra safe with food and drink.

Smoking, and I'm talking tobacco, is an issue that will be up to the studio and the participants. More and more indoor environments are becoming smoke free, and the recording studio is one that could benefit the most from this policy as they are sealed up tightly and smoke can have an adverse effect on the equipment. Some studios will allow smoking in the recording room and not in the control room, some may provide a smoking lounge, and some may ask you to step outside. If smoking is allowed in the studio, as with eating or drinking, be careful. Ashes and other debris can play havoc with recording equipment. Make sure you know the policy of the studio and the preference of the other participants before lighting up.

Don't punch each other! You think I'm kidding? I recently spoke to an engineer in a major East Coast studio who related to me a tale in which two bandmembers got into a shoving fight and threw each other around the recording room a bit before their session was inevitably called to a halt. Fortunately, no injuries were incurred to people or equipment but it was still very bad form. Nothing productive was accomplished at that session.

Get your differences worked out beforehand and leave the personal stuff outside. No good can come from heated arguments in the studio environment. Creative differences can easily come up during a session, but they should be dealt with in the calmest way possible. Very often this is where the role of the producer as the overall creative director comes into play.

It's not a party! If you wish to invite a few interested parties to observe the session, fine, but let them know that they should observe and that's it. Inviting a large number of guests, or allowing even a few guests to get in the way, verbally or physically, will usually result in slowing down the process and distracting the participants.

Don't touch the equipment! Even if you are experienced with studio gear, unless invited by staff members, don't assume you should be pushing buttons, twisting knobs, adjusting mics, or laying your mitts on any part of the studio's equipment. Very often the only pieces of the studio's equipment the staff wants the artists to handle are the headphones they will be wearing in the recording room. This are two reasons for this. First, the studio staff assume that none but they know how they want their equipment to be handled; and second, as soon as you take something in your hands, you become responsible for it. It may seem quicker to adjust the mic that is right in front of you rather than waiting for the assistant to come in from the control room to do it. The problem comes when you give it a little twist and the thing falls over and hits the floor with a resounding thud. You may have just bought a $2500 microphone! If anyone is going to break anything, let it be the staff.

The lifeguard says, "No Running!" Take it easy as you move about the studio. Very often recording rooms become a jungle of stands, wires, instruments, sound baffles, and baffled performers. Even a very small change in the position of a microphone, caused by a bump or shove, can profoundly alter the sound you worked for a hour to get. If you absolutely must leap into the air and do your windmill moves to get the right sound during your solo, let the staff know and they will make room for you...or tie you down.

One last area of studio behavior: Keep your session moving. I have seen many sessions slowly grind down to the point where almost nothing is getting done. Try to stay focused on the work at hand. At some point during your session, people may start to get tired, discouraged, or their attention may start to drift. This may be the right time to take a break and leave the control room for a few minutes. I find that a well-timed break in the action can keep everyone fresher than insisting on continuous activity. A break may be a good idea, but don't let it last too long. A cup of coffee or even a walk around the block can be the right medicine to relieve the claustrophobia of being sealed up in a recording studio for hours at a time, but too long a break will interrupt the flow of your session. Take breaks, get refreshed, and then get back to work.

In all other aspects of studio behavior, using common sense will usually do the trick. There is no need to be overly nervous about every action, but you are in a specialized environment. Don't treat the facility like your rec room, and if you are in doubt about an activity, ask. Follow these simple guidelines, and you will get along just fine with the studio staff.

LAYING DOWN TRACKS

This is the point at which the actual process of putting sound onto tape begins. The musicians have set up and tuned their instruments. The studio staff have gotten good clean signals from each source, either by microphone or direct.

The producer and engineer have agreed that the basic level and tonal quality of the instruments, as heard by the multitrack recorder, are acceptable. If the producer of the project is also going to be playing on the session, he or she will have to do a bit of running back and forth between control room and recording room to make sure everything is OK. Everything is set to go. HOLD IT!!! (Sound of screeching brakes.)

Before going any further with this section, I want to stress one subject: keeping your instruments in tune. The importance of tuning was re-etched in my brain during a recent session. I was acting as producer on a recording when I was asked to add some guitar tracks to what the bandmembers had laid down. The playing posed no problem, as I am an inspired and versatile instrumentalist (gag!). What *was* a problem was trying to get my instrument in tune with the other instruments on the recording. The tuning of the other previously recorded guitars did not agree with the tuning of the bass, and the bass was out of tune to itself. When I say "out of tune to itself," I mean that the intonation of the instrument was so off that it was noticeable. (Intonation is explained in Chapter 1, "Your Equipment.")

I spent an unreasonable amount of time trying to get a tuning on my guitar that would work. It would sound good on one part of the song and terrible on another. The engineer and I even tried altering the speed of the multitrack playback during different sections of the song. In the end, we achieved a satisfactory result but at a great cost in time.

I can't count how many good recordings I have heard that were ruined by lousy tuning. Either the end result sounded sour or it made overdubbing very difficult. All this can be easily avoided if the performers have their instruments' intonation checked and set before the sessions and if they take the care to check their tuning between each take. I will repeat this: Check your tuning between each take.

All types of tunings are possible on stringed instruments. There are even interesting dissonant effects that can be created by purposely putting an instrument out of tune (de-tuning). Whatever tuning is used, it is the responsibility of the performers to ensure that it remains consistent throughout the session. As modern musicians, we have the advantage of having cheap portable tuners available to us. These should be used conscientiously. Even a nonstandard tuning can be kept to consistent values with an accurate electronic tuner. If you are using a nonstandard tuning or are de-tuning your instruments in some way, make a note of this on the track sheet that the engineer is keeping with your multitrack tape. This way, if you want to overdub other instruments at a later date, there will be no guessing as to the tunings used at the previous sessions. Pay attention to your tuning, and your recording will sound better and your overdub and mix sessions will be easier. OK, on to the sessions.

Most modern recording procedures involve the use of multitrack recording, hence, the process known as "laying down tracks." Multitrack recorders are, in theory, just like the stereo tape recorders we use at home but with more tracks. A stereo recorder uses two discrete channels, or tracks, to record and play back the left and right channels that make up a stereo recording. These tracks can also be thought of as one and two, rather than left and right. If you were to increase the number of tracks beyond two, you would enter the realm of multitrack recorders.

Multitrack recorders are special in one other important way: No matter how many tracks a recorder may have, each one can be accessed individually. In other words, tracks 1, 3, 7, and 9 can be playing back while tracks 11 and 12 are recording. The machine can perform these functions so that all the music is in sync. In this way, an artist can play along with previously recorded material and have the new material recorded in sync. If an instrument is properly isolated on its own track, it can also selectively be removed or replaced without disturbing the other tracks. In this way, a mistake by one member of an ensemble can be corrected without having to re-record the entire piece. On an 8-track recorder, I could record eight different guitar parts at different times and play them all back together. This technique, known as "overdubbing," is what ushered in the age of modern multitrack recording.

Multitrack recording was pretty much invented by the Thomas Edison of modern music, Lester William Polfuss, better known as Les Paul. Yes, the same Les Paul whose name is on the famous guitars by Gibson. He constructed the first 8-track recorder in his garage in the 1950s and for awhile had the only one in the world. The earliest commercially produced multitrack recorders used three tracks and were used by such legendary artists as the Beach Boys to produce incredibly complicated recordings. As the creative demands of artists increased, so did the number of tracks available on commercial multitrack recorders. From three tracks to the current common usage of sixty-four tracks in large commercial studios to the use of one-hundred-twenty-eight for the most complicated soundtracks for major motion pictures, multitrack recording has come a long way. If the studio has the right equipment and you have enough money, you can have the luxury of an almost unlimited number of tracks.

No matter how many tracks you have in the studio you use, you will probably lay down basic tracks and then add or overdub others. In many cases, the rhythm section, drums, or percussion with other rhythm instruments are the first to be recorded. This is done because the rhythm instruments set the tempo of the piece, and it is easier for the rest of the band to follow the drummer than vice versa. When each instrument is recorded separately, you can achieve greater isolation between tracks and maintain greater flexibility to correct, add, or delete recorded material. When I say "recorded separately," I don't mean that each instrument must necessarily play solo. What happens is that each instrument is recorded on its own track, or in the case of complex instruments such as drum sets, several tracks. That way, the sounds of that instrument are as isolated as possible from the other sounds on the tape.

Several instruments can play at the same time and still produce isolated tracks by putting amplifiers, or the performers themselves, in separate small rooms called iso (short for isolation) booths with their instruments and microphones. The signals from these different sources are assigned to the tracks on the multitrack recorder chosen for them by the producer or engineer. This assignment is accomplished by means of switches on the mixing desk. More than one instrument can be recorded on each track, but once they are recorded together they can not be separated later. Because of this fact, producers and engineers will try to record each instrument on a track all by itself if the recorder has enough tracks for all the different parts.

The instruments will almost always be recorded dry, or without effects such as reverb or delay. If an effect is recorded to tape, it cannot be removed and is difficult to alter in the mix later on. If you record a guitar part with what sounds like a really awesome, huge reverb and then decide later that there is too much reverb, tough. Now that it's on tape you're stuck with it. Any type of effect the studio can hook up can be, and is usually better off being, added in the mix. Some effects may be recorded because they change the way a part is played. Whether or not an effect is to be recorded should be decided by the musicians and the producer or engineer.

Don't think that if you have, say, sixteen tracks you have enough space for sixteen isolated instruments or voices. Let's look at typical track assignments for our five-piece group—drums, bass, guitar, sax, keys, and vocals. The drums will usually use a minimum of four tracks: one each for bass drum, snare drum, left overhead and right overhead. This is done because the sounds of the bass and snare drums are critical to the sound of the set, and the producer will want to manipulate them separately in the mix. One track each for bass and sax. Two tracks each for guitar and keys. Two tracks each? Hey, who do they think they are hogging all those tracks! Sorry, but if you want instruments with the potential for stereo spread, like modern keys and guitars with effects, they need one track each for the right and left channels of their signals. Now, add three tracks for lead and stereo background vocals, and the group has already used thirteen tracks! I have not even considered doubling vocal or instrumental parts, harmony parts, etc. You can see how easily one can get into track trouble—"Gee, there aren't any tracks left for the sackbut solo"—if one is not careful about track assignment and usage. This should be worked out by the producer and the engineer after they know the total amount of different sounds to be recorded for a particular piece. It is always a good idea to try and leave at least one track open for later inspiration.

The signals generated by each sound source are mixed in the control room by the engineer to form a special monitor mix, and all the performers are able to listen to each other and themselves over headphones. In this way, a group can play together and still get good isolation. The more isolated a track is, the easier it is to mess with later on.

The headphone mix is a very important part of getting good tracks down on tape. The engineer, in most cases, has specific and separate controls for the headphone, or monitor, mix. Anyone in the control room can talk to the musicians through their headphones via the talkback system. There may even be the possibility of more than one monitor mix. The capability for multiple monitor mixes is useful for giving different players levels that work well for them individually. The drummer may want more bass in his mix than the vocalist or guitar player. Most professional studios have the ability to dish out at least two separate mixes for headphone monitoring. Unless a session is unusually large, two mixes can do a good job of satisfying the musicians' requirements.

The performers should get a reasonable balance of the other players and be able to hear themselves clearly, all at a bearable volume. Many studios can even add such basic effects as reverb and delay to the monitor mixes; ask if they can. I am emphasizing so strongly what may seem like a relatively unimportant detail because my personal experience as both a musician and a producer/engineer has taught me that when performers have a really good sounding monitor mix, they play better. This is a law. Artists who are struggling to hear themselves or the other players will not be able to do their best. Asking for different levels of instruments or basic effects in the monitor mix is not bugging the engineer. Don't spend all day on it, but get a headphone mix that everyone is happy with.

Let's say that our fictional five-piece group is going to record a song in the same basic way that they play it on-stage. They might want to play together to keep the feel they know but still be able to go over any flubs later. The studio engineer and the producer will decide how best to set up the group in the facility in order to get good isolation and still allow the band as much of a natural feeling as possible. It can get very weird and claustrophobic if every one is stuck in their own little soundproof room looking at each other through windows. It is quite common to have the members of the band set up in the same larger room and get isolation through the use of gobos. Gobos are moveable room dividers that studios use to either absorb or bounce sound in a particular direction. A good amount of isolation can be preserved in this way, and the band can still be in the same room.

Many times a group laying down basic tracks will play together trying to get good rhythm tracks only. The members of the band are all playing together, but the producer is listening to the bass and drums more carefully than the other instruments. If a version of a song with a really good rhythm track is recorded, the group can always record lead guitar, keyboards, vocals, or anything else they decide on, later. If you are going to use this type of session plan, the producer and the group should be aware of this, so if the guitar player pulls a clanger during a run through, they won't stop playing and possibly ruin an otherwise good take.

Whatever session plan you and your producer decide on, it is my firm belief that the recording process should not prevent the performers from feeling relaxed and good about what they are doing. I have witnessed sessions that were dominated by the needs of the studio to the detriment of the performances. I have also been party to sessions in which the performers hampered the ability of the studio staff to produce the best they could because of an ill-educated or unreasonable viewpoint. Neither of these situations will ever render the finest results. The best sessions are a graceful cooperation between technology and humanity.

OVERDUBBING

The overdubs will be added after the producer is satisfied that a good set of basic tracks for a song have been laid down. If our five-piece group wants a particular section of a song to contain both rhythm and lead guitar, the guitarist will have to play one part or the other as an overdub. Vocal parts are almost always recorded as the last part of the overdubs, to give the vocalists the chance to interact with all of the music that will appear in the final version.

There is nothing very difficult about overdubbing for the artists except getting used to performing alone while listening to the previously recorded tracks. It is not rare for performers to get shy during overdubs. They are alone in the recording room, or iso booth, while the rest of the band and the studio staff are watching and listening to what the performer is doing. The spotlight is on. Even very experienced players can find this nerve wracking. Jimi Hendrix was known to be so shy about laying down vocal overdubs that he insisted that the recording room lights be turned off and gobos be put between himself and the control room so that he could not be seen. It is a good idea to assume that your performers will suffer from the same type of nervousness, to some degree, during overdubs. Try to get them set up in the recording room so that they do not see seven or eight pairs of eyes staring at them every time they look up. Turning the lights down and facing them away from the control room window will help them concentrate on what they are doing. Even if they can't see the control room, you can still communicate through the talkback system.

Some types of overdubs can even be done right in the control room. There have been several occasions when I have recorded electronic keyboard parts while sitting at the mixing desk. An electronic keyboard doesn't require an amplifier or microphones to be recorded. The signal can be taken directly to the mixing desk and can be easier and quicker to set up in the control room. If the player is comfortable with this, don't be surprised if the engineer suggests that this be done. They are trying to save you time.

During overdubbing, you have the opportunity to fix any mistakes, or change sections of a track, without re-recording the entire part. This technique is known as punching-in. Modern multitrack recorders have the ability to start and stop recording on an almost instantaneous basis. This gives the players time to correct mistakes as small as a single note. I would go after and correct anything you hear that is bothering you, like errant noises. It will bother you every time you hear it afterwards. The time needed to do this is well worth it. If clangers are on your final mix, everyone else will assume you or your group either couldn't play the songs well or didn't care enough to fix them.

Recording punch-ins is just like doing overdubs, except that a very small section will be recorded to replace the original material on the original track, rather than on a separate track. The engineer must take care to replace only the part required or you might lose something you want to keep. The performer will hear the playback of the song. When the section to be replaced is reached, the multitrack recorder, either by automatic or manual trigger, will switch from playback to record mode on the track specified. The performer is aware of which part to play or sing again and simply does so at the appropriate point. This sounds easy and usually is. Some punch-ins can make you tear your hair out, though. The position of the section to be replaced, what comes immediately before and after, can make some punch-ins very difficult for both the performers and the engineer. If a particular punch-in is proving to be problematic, the best solution is to try and punch-in a slightly longer section, one with small silent spaces at the beginning and end of the punch-in. This gives the equipment and the performer a little time to get in and out of the track smoothly.

The overdubbing part of the sessions is the last time it will be easy to change or add something to the tracks. After overdubbing is complete, the chances are that your and the studio's equipment will be removed from the recording room and the control room equipment will be re-patched for mixing. Make sure that you have done all that you want to the tracks before declaring overdubbing finished. If you have prepared a list of things to add or fix, make sure that everything has been covered. When you and the producer are satisfied with the tracks, it is time to progress to the final mix. Now the fun begins!

THE MIX SESSIONS

The purpose of the mix session is deceptively simple to describe: To set the levels, tonal qualities, and position (left, right, or center) of all the tracks that will appear in the final stereo version of the piece. Sounds fine, should be done in an hour or two. Hold on there, Tonto. What sounds simple can be quite complicated to achieve.

The producer, engineer, and perhaps, but not always, the artists must make many decisions that can have a drastic effect on how a finished piece of music sounds. During the mix session, you have the opportunity to delete or mute tracks completely or in part. You can decide how loud a particular instrument will be in relation to the others. The tonal qualities of everything record-ed can be radically altered. Any electronic effect you or the studio possess can be added to recorded tracks. The final kicker is the ability to cut up and rearrange the piece as a whole if this is desired.

Some mix sessions I have done were a breeze. The producer and artists agreed on the overall direction the recording would take from the beginning, and all the parts recorded were planned with the final mix in mind. Very little fixing and fiddling had to be done to get an exciting and dynamic final mix. Other mix sessions have been close to nightmares. Entire bands arguing about what should be "up front" or loudest in the mix, parts being taken out and then replaced, requests being made that could not be accommodated because the material had not been recorded with the request in mind (remember recording too much reverb on the guitar track?), frustration and disappoint-ment setting in because of a lack of vision.

The producer and engineer should be free to sit at the mixing desk and work and think. They should not be physically or mentally crowded. To the uninitiated, it might not seem like a lot is going on, but they do have a lot to concentrate on. Remaining focused on a song, perhaps for hours at a time, is not an easy job. Even if the artist is included in the production team for final mix, they would be wise to listen and learn. You must assume that the produc-er and engineer are working well within your plans. If you feel something major is happening to your music that you don't like, then of course you should speak up. Most of the time, producers and engineers have spent a lot more time in studios than artists. And if the artists' wishes have been clearly stated, then it is best to let the pros do their stuff. If they are any good, the pro-ducer and engineer should ask the artists questions all along the way.

One decision that will need to be made, and it can be a thorny one, is who should be present at the mix session. The producer and engineer have the pivotal roles in mix sessions. In fact, some major label artists trust their pro-ducers to the point of not even being present during mix sessions. This does not work for everyone, and most of the time the artist will want to be present to have a say in what is going on. This is fine up to a point. The problems arise when a group of four or five, or more, musicians all want to be present and all want to have a say. There can be dozens of decisions to make during the mix of only one song. If all those decisions are to made by committee, the process becomes impossibly slow. What to do?

If a musical group is paying for a recording together, as is commonly the case, how do you tell the members to butt out and let the producer get down to business? Very gently. Bandmembers should not necessarily be excluded from mix sessions, but if they have not been chosen as producer or co-producer, they should be informed that they now take on the role of observers. If they have not been involved in mix sessions before, they should be told that the process may quickly become tedious and boring for them as the track is played over and over to try different mixes and root out any problems.

This sounds like I am trying to discourage bandmembers from attending mix sessions. You're right, I am. It is my experience that most mixes benefit from having as few opinions as possible. Every member of a band will want to protect their track. They will want it as loud and as bright as possible because, to them, what they played is the most important part of the piece. This is obviously not true. Everything cannot be the most important part at the same time. Decisions have to be made concerning the prominence of some parts over others. This is where the role of the producer becomes most important and perhaps most difficult. Someone must be the final judge of what is good in a mix, and this should be the producer. If you chose your producer wisely and communicated well, there should not be any great differences of opinion this late in the process. The producer should be able to shepherd the recording and all the egos involved, to a completion that satisfies most if not all.

By this time, you should be able to get a good mix session under your belt and, by rights, have a good mix. It is time to progress to the post-mix menu of options. Double click on the next chapter and let's see what happens.

Chapter 6

The Final Product

You are excited. Your producer and the engineer are smiling and nodding approval. Interested observers are congratulating you. Your mix is done and it is good. It's better than good, it is transcendental. Time to go out and collect sacks of money, the respect of your peers, the accolades of a generation, and the approval of your parents. Wait a minute. There are still a few things you will need to do in and out of the studio before getting your slice of genius into the sweating palms of the waiting masses.

THE FINISHED MASTER

At this point, let's separate the two masters you will end up with. The finished mixes you complete in the recording studio are your source masters, while what a mastering engineer will produce is a master. OK? When you produce your source master in a recording studio, the expression used is to "mix to 2-track." In the case of surround sound mixing, a multitrack recording is mixed to a recorder with more than 2-tracks, but most recording artists will be mixing to a 2-track stereo recorder.

The finished mix will be printed on a 2-track (stereo) format, and that will be your source master. You will need to choose what mastering format you wish to use. Almost all studios I know of mix to a tape format of some kind. Many studios have more than one type of 2-track recorder available. Although hard drive, direct to CD, and minidisc recorders are available, few studios use them as a mastering format on a regular basis. The most common formats to use for a 2-track mix are reel-to-reel and DAT (digital audio tape). It makes very good sense to use a common format when mixing so that the finished source master can be used by as many facilities as possible. Even if you own a minidisc recorder, I would not use that as your only source mastering format, because you may not find that type of machine in use at all other facilities.

Analog reel-to-reel tape, although seemingly old-fashioned in this day of digital everything, is still widely used in the professional recording industry. Many artists and producers prefer the sound of analog tape over digital formats, and many major artists and studios still mix to reel-to-reel. These machines bear little resemblance to the home reel-to-reel recorders of years ago. They have very large (10.5-inch) reels of tape that run at double or even quadruple the speed of home recorders, and their sound quality, if the machine is properly maintained, is superb. The advantages of studio reel-to-reel recorders are that they produce very stable recordings, give you the ability to edit the tape physically, and are widely used in the industry. The disadvantages are that they use large and expensive reels of tape and the machines themselves are very expensive and not found in other than professional environments.

DAT recorders are audio tape recorders that translate sound signals into streams of computer-generated numbers; then those numbers are recorded onto a very small, slowly moving cassette tape. The DAT cassette is completely different from a regular audio cassette, except that it also uses magnetic tape. If you are going to use DAT as a source master format, don't bring a regular audio cassette and expect to use it in a DAT machine. It won't fit.

Like all digital audio formats, the advantages of DAT are that it adds virtually no background noise, provides a huge dynamic range, and has no signal distortion or coloration due to tape anomalies. DAT tapes are also small, inexpensive, and widely available. You can get a 120-minute DAT tape in almost any Radio Shack for under $15. Compare this to paying $40 or more for a reel of professional reel-to-reel mastering tape available only from pro tape suppliers. Years ago, I heard of complaints from other studio professionals about DAT tapes and recorders sometimes producing unstable results. I have used DAT as a mastering format for years and have never had trouble with it. The main disadvantages of DAT are that the sound is sometimes criticized as "cold," and the tape cannot be edited manually. If you want to swap the order of the songs, you have to make a DAT-to-DAT copy and change the order when you do. Most recording studios can do this for you.

DAT is in wide use in the professional recording industry. Unlike other pro formats, it is also found in the consumer market. DAT was originally sold as a consumer product but was quickly embraced by professional audio engineers as a cost effective and extremely accurate source mastering format. The consumer market for DAT never really took off, but DAT recorders and their tapes are available in almost every well-stocked consumer electronic store. This is very cool for musicians. Before DAT, the source mastering formats used by recording studios used equipment that was far beyond the economic means of almost all home users. With the advent of DAT, a format accurate enough for recording studios to use was now also affordable enough for the consumer to buy. DAT machines are not cheap (starting at around $500), but they are a lot cheaper than pro reel-to-reel recorders (starting at around $2500). For all these reasons, DAT machines have finally bridged the gap between pro and home formats.

Why is this important? Before DAT, a finished studio source master could not be played, in its original form, on anything other than studio equipment. To be able to play your source master, to make a few copies on cassette, say, one had to go back to a studio or use a professional tape duplicating house. This is not necessarily true with DAT. Many DAT machines are in use in artists' homes, radio stations, small studios, and professional tape duplicating facilities. It may even be within your personal finances to purchase a DAT recorder to be able to make cassette copies at home. Although this would not work for large-scale duplication, it sure does make it possible to be able to play your finished masters in the original pristine form in many places other than recording studios.

Looks like I am making a pretty strong case for using DAT as a source mastering format. I see DAT as being the most cost effective, convenient, and perhaps the best sounding of the commonly available mastering formats. Even if you use another mastering format, I would also get a copy on DAT. I would always get more than one copy of any masters in any format for safety's sake. Many hours of work and lots of money is tied up in your master, and it would be a minor tragedy to lose all of that because the only copy got beer spilled on it. Extra copies of finished masters are called "safety copies" in the industry. More than one safety is not a bad idea.

Until recently, the economics of making a CD of a recording limited this format to commercial runs of 500 copies or more. This is no longer the case. Machines that record onto blank CDs one at a time are now available. These machines cost upward of $3000 and so are not affordable to the average home user, but they have opened up other options for the recording musician. Duplicating houses can now produce single CDs from a master tape for as little as $35 each. Businesses that specialize in this service advertise in most popular musicians' and recording magazines.

It would be a good idea for those of you who cannot afford to release your recording on CD to get a few individual copies of your source master on this format. This will give you a digital version of your master on a very common home format. For very important promotional editions of your recording, a CD offers the best sound quality, and a CD of your source master is the perfect source to make home cassette copies from.

The chances are that you will be sending one copy of your master to a professional tape duplicating company to have cassette copies or CDs made. I would hate sending my only copy of a master through the mail to a facility that may be hundreds, if not thousands, of miles away. I get a warm, fuzzy feeling having multiple copies of my masters.

The source master is the version of your recording from which all distribution copies will be made. Whether those copies are to made on cassettes, CDs, vinyl, or whatever, the source master will be the source. Because of this, your master tapes are very special and worthy of special care. Leaving one copy of a master tape for safekeeping with the studio is considered fairly standard practice. Even if the copies you take with you all get lost or destroyed, the one stored at the studio could save you from having to remix. Almost all serious studios have a special storage area to keep clients' finished multitrack and source master tapes. Unless you have a way to keep your valuable studio tapes safe from kids, pets, floods, etc., you might do well to let the studio keep them for you. If this is not convenient for you, consider your storage options carefully. A basement closet is not a good place for your multitrack or master tapes to reside. Choose a place that is cool, dry, away from direct sunlight, and unlikely to be disturbed by anyone other than you. A bank safe deposit box is one of the safest options. They are affordable and not usually subject to the ravages of flood, fire, or peanut butter.

One last word of advice about master tapes: Don't lend them out. If your friend has a DAT recorder and wants to hear your latest opus in all its digital glory, make them a copy. The master from the recording studio is worth much more than the price of the tape. Most people do not realize how valuable a master tape is to the artist and do not treat them with the proper respect. Keep your master tapes under your control, and you will not have to be running back to the studio wasting time and money to have more copies made.

MASTERING

For all release formats, a certain amount of "mastering" is involved in turning a source master into a consumer format. Mastering is a term that is often misunderstood. I admit it is inherently confusing to have a master tape and then have to master it to turn it into another format. One use of the word is as a noun; the other is as a verb.

Using the word "master" as a verb comes from the days when all commercial releases were in the form of records. A master disk was produced by playing the audio tape of a performance through a master cutting lathe that made a needle cut grooves that corresponded to the electrical signals into a master disk. This disk was the reference to which all the subsequent copies should conform. Hence, it was a master. The process to create it became known as mastering.

The person whose specialty it is to know all the ins, outs, and audio tricks that can be involved in turning a good source master into a great master is the mastering engineer. This person's job is to do everything they can to make your source master sound as good or better than the original once it is copied onto a release format (CD, cassette, etc.). In the world of major label artists, the mastering engineer is a star in their own right and is many times considered important enough to have an album credit. Most of the people who read this book will not have the kind of budget necessary to hire "star" mastering engineers, but you would still be wise to pay close attention to the mastering process and to choose a quality facility. It would be a shame for your carefully produced recording to get muddied up in mastering and copying.

Even though you may not be making vinyl records of your recording, the process involved in turning your recording into a home format is still called mastering. I will not go into the technical aspects of mastering for each format, but some general rules apply. If you have contracted with your producer to take your recording through the mastering process, all the better. They should be able to tell the duplicating company what you want. Your producer should also be able to judge if the copies are being turned out properly. If your producer is not going this far with you or you are self producing your project, read on.

Organize your source masters from the recording studio! Before you send your finished mixes to a facility to be mastered to a release format, get all of your ducks in a row. One of the classic ways to waste the time of your mastering engineer, and your money in the process, is to send a box of unlabeled tapes to the mastering lab and expect them to figure out where the right takes are. I have actually heard of source masters from national artists showing up at mastering facilities unlabeled and thrown in a box. The mastering engineers then had to spend hours reviewing each tape and calling the artist to make sure they were working on the correct version of each song. Don't do this! Putting a mastering engineer through this kind of hair pulling will cost you money and lots of time. The process of deciding how your songs will appear on your final release is called editing.

Editing is better undertaken in the recording studio than in the mastering lab. Editing is the process of deciding which mixes you want to include on your release, in what order you want them to appear, and what length of silent spaces you want in between songs. Thousands of years ago, when humans recorded in caves with stone knives and bearskins, editing was performed with razor blades and paper leader tape. Now that we are all masters/victims of the computer age, your editing will probably take place at a computer workstation. No matter. With whichever format you are using to send your finished mixes to the mastering lab—DAT, minidisc, CD-R, or reel-to-reel—make sure that you make yourself a cassette tape with your songs in the order that you would like them to appear on your release with the proper blank spaces in between.

Space: the final frontier. After you have spent many hours arguing with your bandmates about the length of spaces between songs and have come to an agonizing compromise, you may find that the mastering lab prefers to have lots of space between songs. If this is the case, talk to them. Give them what will work well for them. Time the spaces you have decided on and include these timings on the log you send to the mastering lab that shows the order of the song titles. If the mastering lab has timings for the blank spaces between songs, they can reproduce what you want.

Take home the copy of your entire prospective release. Live with this collection for a while. If you want to make changes, now is the time. If you are satisfied with the order and timing of your collected recordings, it is time to go on to the mastering engineer.

The recording that you send to the mastering lab should have absolutely no sound on it that you do not wish to appear on your release. If the chosen mix of your magnum opus has an errant note or sound at the beginning or end, remove it before you send your recording to be mastered. This is called "topping and tailing." Once this is done, the true running time of a song is known and should be logged. It is true that the mastering lab can change the order of the songs, set the position and length of blank spaces, and clean up spurious noises for the release master, but they will have to spend extra time to do this and will charge you for it. You also have much more flexibility to change things in the recording studio than when working with a mastering lab where you probably will not be present.

Make a log. Put that chainsaw away, Paul Bunyan! I mean a written log that will show the mastering engineer, in a clear manner, which songs are to appear, in what order, and with how much blank space between each. Such a log might look like this:

Artist: The Big Stinkers
Phone: (999) 888-7777
Contact: Bob
Album Title: Stink With Me
Song Sequence:
1   "I Have a Stripe Down My Back" (3:45)
    (From DAT #2, Cut #5)
    (4 Sec. blank)
2   "Pepe La Pue's Blues" (4:45)
    (From DAT #1, Cut #7)
    (3.5 Sec. blank)
3   "Dumpster Diver's Delight" (2:56)
    (From DAT #3, Cut #4)
And so on...

The above example assumes that the artist is sending source masters on DAT. Other formats—reels, minidiscs, etc., should be indicated and marked accordingly. Other special instructions to the mastering engineer should be included at the end of the log or on an attached sheet. Even if you have talked to the mastering engineer about your project, I would include all instructions in writing with your source tapes. Written reminders help to assure that nothing gets forgotten.

See that the source tapes or disks you send are properly and clearly labeled so that the mastering engineer can quickly and easily find the proper cuts for your release. Each source tape or disc should not only include song titles, organized by number with running times, but should also have at least the artist's name and phone number on the tape or disc and its box or sleeve. It is of almost no use at all to have meticulous labeling on boxes or sleeves if you cannot tell which tape goes with which box once they have been separated. Your name and phone number should be on everything, just in case one piece gets separated from the whole package. Have at least one safety copy of every tape or disc you send just in case something gets lost. Ask your recording engineer for safety copies of your finished mixes. They will be able to provide them for very little money. A very good investment.

If you are going to send a sequenced source master—a tape that is set up exactly how the release is to sound, all songs and all spaces—let your mastering lab know this and ask if there are any special things they would like you to do. A sequenced master must be perfect from beginning to end, so don't think you can just throw one together. There is nothing wrong or unusual in sending a fully sequenced source master to a mastering lab, but most people leave the sequencing to the mastering lab. If you decide to produce your own fully sequenced source master, avoid radical re-EQing, compression, or other major massaging of your mixes. The mastering lab will have to do some, or all, of these things to your source master to help it shine brightly when reproduced. In all cases, send the mastering lab the cleanest, most dynamically open source master possible. Let them take it from there with your guidance.

When the mastering engineer is finished with their work, they will send the completed masters to the duplicating house of your choice. Many times the mastering lab is a part of the duplicating company, and no shipping is needed. If you are using separate mastering and duplicating facilities, it is best to let them transfer the completed master without sending it to you first. (This cuts down on the middlemen.)

RELEASE FORMATS/DUPLICATION

Once you have your completed master, with the songs and spaces in the order you want, it is time to copy it to a release format. A release format is the type of copy you will be putting into the hands of the general public, agents, record companies, your friends and family. The decision about which release format(s) you will use, should be based on popularity of use, sound quality, the number of copies to be made, your budget, and style. The most commonly used release formats are audio cassettes, compact discs, and, yes, vinyl. That's right, records. Let's look at these three formats one at a time. I will call these home music formats as opposed to professional formats.

Audio cassettes have proven to be one of the most popular and venerable of home audio formats. Almost everyone has a cassette player, and some of them are of very good quality. You really can't go wrong if you decide to release your recording on cassettes. They are easy and inexpensive to reproduce in quantity and are small and lightweight to mail. Sounds perfect. End of decision, right? Not quite. Although audio cassettes have some decided virtues, they also have some distinct drawbacks.

The first of these is sound quality. In comparison to the other two home release formats I mentioned, audio cassettes come in last in sound quality. The way the tape is used in this format just does not allow a sound recording to be reproduced with the same accuracy and fidelity of CDs or even well-pressed vinyl. Why are cassettes so popular then? Because they are cheap and do a reasonably good job of reproducing audio. Cassettes also became very popular because of their use in auto and portable radio/tape players.

If you are an independent artist with a limited budget, trying to get the most copies for your dollars, then cassettes are probably the way to go, especially if you are considering a limited run of under a thousand copies. You can still get good audio response at a good price. There are ways to make cassettes even less expensive than the ones you see packaged in music stores. Most of those are in clear plastic boxes with nice artwork and the song titles printed on the cassette itself. Those clear boxes are called Norelco boxes in the industry and are the industry standard for commercial release of audio cassettes. They are not the only type of boxes available. What are known as soap dish boxes and even cardboard sleeves can also be used and at less cost. The problem is that these other boxes scream cheap to everyone and only save a few pennies per copy. I would avoid using them, if at all possible.

When making cassette copies, you will have a choice between making high-speed or real-time copies. When you send your master to a cassette duplicating company, they load your master into a playback machine that is hooked up to many cassette recorders. These machines, the playback machine and the recorders, can be synched to operate at a higher than normal speed, thereby cutting down the time for the company to make, say, one hundred cassette copies of your master. The only problem is that audio quality suffers quite a bit. In real-time mode, the master is played, the recorders record at normal speed, and the greatest amount of fidelity is preserved. It may seem very tempting to save a few dollars by having high-speed copies made, but you may be disappointed with the results. I know that I do not want to work in a recording studio for all that time and spend all that money trying to get the best possible sound quality, only to have it muddied up trying to save a few bucks in copying.

You will also need to make a decision about what type of tape is going to be used in your cassettes. The basic types in use today are, in ascending order of cost, normal bias, high bias, and metal bias tape. In most cases, I find that good-quality high bias tape yields very satisfactory results without breaking the bank. Normal bias tape will sound noisy and lack treble response. Metal tape, although technically better than high bias, is quite a bit more expensive and requires a tape machine with special playback features to reveal the full superiority of the format. Many tape players are not equipped to properly play back metal tapes. Because of usage, sound quality, and cost, I would recommend using high bias tape copied at real-time speed.

The audio cassette and the compact disc format are the current industry standards for commercial release. CDs are a home digital music reproduction format and are very good at what they do. CDs offer audio reproduction that is virtually free of noise and distortion. They are reasonably small, easy to transport, and in the last few years have become remarkably inexpensive to reproduce. When made in amounts of one thousand or more, they are quite competitive in cost to cassettes and offer much better quality. CD players are, like cassette players, everywhere.

The CDs you see in stores are packaged in what are known as jewel boxes. CDs can also be ordered from manufacturers in light plastic envelopes that are less expensive to buy and ship. Many large music companies use these envelopes to package their promotional copies. I have never seen CDs for sale with this type of packaging, however. If you are going to offer your CDs for sale, I would stick with the jewel boxes. Even though they are a little more expensive, jewel boxes protect your product better and are what people expect to see when they buy a CD.

The only real drawback to releasing your recording on CD is cost. CDs cost more than cassettes to copy. Although they are more expensive, the difference in quality more than justifies the cost. CDs only become really cost effective when reproduced in numbers of a thousand or more. There are services that will turn your master into a compact disc in quantities as small as one, but the cost per unit is high. Like all manufactured products, the cost per unit goes down when greater numbers are made. If your budget allows, I would give CD release some serious thought.

Records. Ah! The golden days of vinyl. I am not waxing nostalgic when I include records as a viable release format. Although you are not likely to see many records in your local Wal-Mart, there is still a lot of new vinyl circulating within the industry. Many club DJs still prefer the sound of records over CDs, and quite a few alternative bands are releasing records as well as other formats because they are, well, alternative. Well-made records can give very high-quality results and are fairly cheap to reproduce. If you are releasing dance music or just like the style of records, they are still a viable release format.

I do not think it is a good idea to release your recording on vinyl alone. Most recordings that are released on record are also available on CD or cassette. If you want to try and crack a specialty market, like club DJs, records should be considered. There are still millions of record players out there and virtually all radio stations still use them. Sending around a record as a demo may even get you a little extra attention. Both LPs and 45s are still being produced.

Whatever format you decide to use for distribution, get the best quality you can afford. If you decide to use a commercial duplicating company, get quotes from several and ask what other artists they have worked with. I would go with reputable companies who can supply a list of references. You would not want to find that even 10 percent of your copies are less than perfect. Commercial duplicating companies regularly advertise in music industry magazines such as *Electronic Musician, Mix*, and *Guitar Player*. If you live in a larger city, there may be a company right in your town. Using a service that is close to where you live can have advantages if there is a problem with the copies. You won't find yourself shipping two hundred bad CDs back to Upper Volta. Look in the phone book or ask the studio where you did your recording if they know of a good duplicating company. Sometimes recording studios will run copying services or have duplicating companies with which they are partnered. They might extend a discount to you as a studio customer.

Even if you are using a reputable duplicating service, I would check a random sample of the copies you get. I would certainly want to be as sure as I could that the copies sound as good as I want them to before I send them out. Ask for a test copy of the format you are choosing to make sure that your recording is being faithfully copied. If, for example, you feel that your test copy lacks the bass response of your master, the duplicating company can adjust the tonal balance to your specifications. Other processing, such as compression, can be applied during the mastering or copying process. If you and the duplicating company decide to process your master in a certain way, get very specific technical information describing what was done. You may not understand the language, but if you decide to have more copies made at a later date, you can make sure that the same processing is applied.

GRAPHICS/ALBUM CREDITS

With whatever format you choose for release, you must give some thought to the packaging. The way your tape, CD, or record appears will have a great effect on its acceptance. The graphics of a package have been credited, in some cases, with selling more copies than the music within. I do not mean to say that the graphics of a release are more important that the music, but the look is very important. Major labels spend a lot, and I mean a lot, of time and money deciding how a release will look. If you have a pile of dough, great! Go out and hire a photographer, graphic artist, art director, manicurist, and stable boy. If you don't have piles of cash, you might have to do a little more leg work, but you can still end up with a quality graphic.

Most people do not have any experience in the field of graphics design. It is certainly not my specialty, but I have picked up a few pointers along the way. Graphics style can give prospective customers and industry people big clues as to the style of your music. Good graphics also tell people that you are serious about the quality of your music. If you were to see a CD with swirling neon colors in a tie-dyed pattern, without ever hearing the recording, you could predict that there would be a certain psychedelic twist to the music therein. When I see elaborate Germanic typefaces used to spell the name of a band, I assume it's some kind of heavy metal music.

This does not mean that if you have recorded a particular style of music you must use graphic styles commonly used with that music. What it does mean is that if you're not careful, you can give people the wrong impression about what is on your recording. In the area of graphics, the "we can do it ourselves" approach almost never works well. Short of going to art school, what are you to do?

Going to art school is one good idea. I don't mean that you should take a course, but it is possible to go to the local art schools in your area and examine the work of the students and even the instructors. Talk to them and find out who might be interested in either creating or having an existing illustration, photograph, painting, etc. used on your release. You may get lucky and find exactly what you're looking for. If you can't find your ideal artists at your local art school or college, you can always ask if any other musicians in your area know of professional graphic artists they have worked with. Make sure that any artwork or photos used are credited on the release and get written permission to use the stuff. It is not cool or legal to use someone else's images without their permission.

This brings up the area of credits and liner notes that will appear with your recording. The credits may be dictated somewhat by agreements that you may have made with the various people who worked on your recording. If you have a signed agreement or even told someone that their name will appear on your release, it had better be there when it is finally printed and released. If not, you'll have some unhappy campers on your hands, who may even be able to sue you. In my opinion, everyone who has made a substantive contribution to the completion of your recording deserves a credit with their name spelled correctly.

In one instance that I can remember, I was acting as audio engineer in a major nightclub in western Massachusetts where a local band was performing as the opening act. They brought a multitrack recorder with them and wanted to hook it up to the club's sound mixer in order to get a multitrack recording of their performance. This is much more complicated than hooking up a simple stereo recorder, and I had to do quite a bit of extra work to connect and operate their recorder during the set. I engineered that recording for them at no cost. I don't mind doing things like this for people just starting out because we all need a hand in the beginning. But I was a bit put out when they subsequently released some of the songs recorded that night and my name was nowhere to be found in the credits. I would be less likely to give those folks a hand in the future.

On the opposite side of the spectrum, I recently brought my multitrack recording rig to two clubs to record a local artist whom I respect both musically and personally. Even though the amount of money I was paid for this service was minimal. I would gladly help this artist again because he included my name, the name of my assistant, and the name of my business on his CD's credits; he also sent me two copies of the CD on which the recordings appeared. He had called me before his CD's release to make sure of the spelling of the names and information. This artist subsequently garnered national attention, and I can prove my connection to his work by means of the album credit.

As you can see, album credits can be quite important to people both personally and professionally. The easiest way to keep track of every person, business, or organization that helps you get your recording finished and released is to keep track as you go along. If you take down the various names, preferably in your trusty project notebook, your information for credits will be accurate and in good shape when you have to tell your printer or graphic artist what you want on your sleeve. Even so, double check the spelling of names. It can be particularly tricky and very embarrassing if you get them wrong.

The credits for a typical recording might read like this for an album by The Couches:

The Couches are:
Jim Squigly—Guitar & Vocals
Fred "Sticks" Shadey—Drums
Red Froggybottom—Bass
Chuck Inaclanger—Keyboards & Vocals

Produced by: Lotta Gutz
Horns on tracks 4, 6 & 7: Ba Fong Gule—Trumpet
Will I. Ever—Sax
Paul Czyrylylzl—Trombone
Piano on track 3: Bud Insky
Recorded at Dripping Slime Studio, Anytown, USA
Recording Engineer: Whey Tu Laud
Assistant Engineer: Unter Pade

The above is pretty much the minimum. If you use photographs, definitely credit the photographer. You might think of crediting your mastering engineer, graphic artist, manager, publicist, and others who are important to the eventual success of your release. If you wish to credit everyone who got sandwiches for you while you were in the studio, please be my guest. Thank yous on releases are a good way to show your appreciation to those who may have made some intangible contribution to your inspiration. You are only limited by space.

The liner notes are separate from the credits, in that this is where someone, usually the artist, gets the chance to rattle on about some silliness that they think has some earth-shattering importance and relevance to the music. If you wish to add liner notes, biographical material, etc., my only advice is to consider carefully what appears on your release. Many different people will read what is written. They will connect this with you, and you will have to live with it for a long time.

Many artists like to include the printed lyrics to their songs as part of the release. If you do this, you must be careful to print only that which you have specific permission from the copyright holder to use, and you must include the proper notice of copyright with the lyrics for each song. If you record someone else's song, you must get written permission from them and their publisher to reprint the lyrics to that song (see Chapter 7, "Copyright Protection").

Many music duplicating companies have in-house graphics departments or artists they recommend. If you are using a duplicating company, ask to see some of the artwork produced for other projects. If you see something you like, the duplicating company can get you in touch with the artist. Many duplicating companies offer package deals that include artwork and typesetting for your release. These deals can be very financially attractive and can work quite well. Always make sure you will get exactly what you want and are not pushed into using a design that may have been sitting on the shelf for a few years. Most graphic artists can work in several different styles, so if you see something that is clean and professional looking but not what you would put on your release, don't write that person off. Find out if they feel they could produce something that would work for you.

CD inserts, cassette "J" cards, and record covers all require special printing and paper-cutting techniques. Even if you do not use the house graphic service of a duplicating company, they should be able to steer you in the right direction to get the actual printing done. Always ask to see a proof of the actual pieces that will be used with your release. Printers, like all of us, are prone to making mistakes. Look everything over very carefully, and then look it over again. Once you give your approval, the misspelling of your name in the credits is your fault, and you will have to pay to have it printed again.

Some things are a given in the area of graphic arts. Like your recording, the more complicated your concept, the more it will cost you. Full color costs more than black and white. Reproducing photographs costs more than simple type and colored backgrounds. A good graphic artist will be able to put together a good look for your release without busting your budget. Getting the right look for your release may take a few meetings with the artist and a few rough drafts, but it is worth it. A good-looking package complements all the hard work you have put into your recording.

Chapter 7

What Now?

This chapter is not intended to provide detailed information on any of the subjects covered, but I felt I would be remiss if I ignored them completely. I am calling attention to the fact that these areas of interest are necessary to complete the process of idea to recording to product. (See RESOURCES chapter for a listing of books that cover, in depth, all the information necessary to become knowledgeable in the following fields.)

RELEASE (COMMERCIAL/INDEPENDENT)

Your baby is now ready to go out into the big wide world, all dressed up in its best graphic clothes and sounding like a million bucks. Are you done? No. The process of getting your recording heard and sold has only just begun. All artists who want to get their recording to the general public will find themselves walking down one of two release roads. Commercial release or independent. Artists in the commercial release category are signed to record labels that are in the business of selling music to the public. Independent release is the category most artists making their first recordings find themselves in.

If you are signed to a record label that has distribution, marketing, advertising, and promotional avenues already set up, you have different concerns than the independent artist. Even though your label may have departments to take care of the details of release, this doesn't mean that you should just sit back and watch. If life was fair, all releases would get the same amount of support from their respective labels. As you probably know by now, though, life is not fair. The music business is rife with tales of really good albums being ignored to death by their releasing labels. How do you prevent this from happening to yours? By being astute, attentive, and hustling your recording within your own label. Even within the halls of your company, you are still the person who cares most about your recording, and you should take an active interest in how well and how much your music is being presented to the public. If you are signed to a label that has multiple releases to take care of, you want to make sure that they are giving the proper attention to yours. You can keep your label excited about your release by the force of your own interest and enthusiasm. Let them know that you want to be involved in all aspects of your recording's release but that you don't intend to be obstructive.

Follow your release through the various levels of your label's personnel. Make every effort to meet with the various people who will be responsible for each activity involved with the release of your work. This may include persons assigned to sales, publicity, public relations, advertising, promotion, merchandising, tour support, and others. I know that everyone does a better job for those with whom they have a good personal relationship. Never ignore this.

If you know little or nothing about the inner workings of record labels, you would be doing yourself a great favor to find out. Even if you are not signed, chances are you would dearly like to be. Your chances of landing a contract go way up the more you know about how the recording business works and what it wants.

Those not signed to a label find themselves in the independent category. Only a few years ago, the era of the independent record label was being pronounced dead or dying by those in the business. The music scene was going to be completely dominated by huge multinational companies that were going to squeeze the life out of all independents. As things have turned out, independent labels have made a strong comeback over the ensuing years and even challenge the majors in specific areas of music. Even large national chains of music retailers have recognized the value of carrying more than just the Top 40 titles in the charts, and there are a multiplicity of mom-and-pop outlets for independent releases.

This does not mean that you will not have to work hard at getting your release noticed. You will. Releasing your own recording is essentially like starting your own record label. As an independent, you will have to provide support in all the same areas that a large label does, only you will have to do this with little or no staff. This may seem like an overwhelming task, but many a famous artist has started with an independent release and risen to world-wide fame.

Take the band Mötley Crüe, for example. They released their first album, *Too Fast for Love*, independently on their own label, Leather Records. This release garnered some local sales and caught the attention of Elektra

Records. That company bought the master, re-released the recording, and signed the band. The band's next release on Elektra sold over three million copies in the United States. Obviously their rise in popularity had a lot to do with having a big record company behind them, but they never would have gotten the attention of Elektra without their independent release.

These types of success stories do not happen by magic or accident. They are the result of many hours of diligent work and patience on someone's part, if not by the artist, then someone working for or with them. There really is no such thing as an overnight success in the music business. Background knowledge and groundwork are necessary to achieve, and more importantly sustain, financial success.

If you expect real economic gain and industry attention, you will need help. Nobody is born with all the skills, knowledge, and contacts needed to shepherd a recording from obscurity to prominence. You will have to develop or seek out marketing skills that will help to have your release stand out from the rest. You will need to get information on distribution, marketing, and sales. These fields are all important in getting those copies of your recording out of the boxes in your basement and into the hands of pleased customers. At the same time, you are going to be trying to get the attention of larger labels, in the hope that they will want to get behind you and your career.

Fortunately for the modern independent, there are many sources of information available that only a few years ago were not. There are volumes of knowledge available in the form of books, cassettes, and video tapes, which offer valuable insight into the details of exploiting your recording. I highly recommend that you avail yourself of as many of these works as you have time and money for. The guidance you receive will allow you to spend your days and greenbacks in the most effective manner.

PROMOTION

Professionals in the music business fully recognize that letting people know that their product exists is all-important in making an impression on a marketplace. If you have the good fortune to be signed to a large record company, they will have separate departments devoted to publicity, promotion, and advertising. Their common goal is to let as many people as possible know that your recording is available and to have them view that recording in a positive light even before they have heard the first note.

If you are unsigned, your goals are not different, you just have to accomplish them without a staff. You have recently completed a sterling sounding recording, had it mastered and reproduced with care, and surrounded the release copies with eye-catching graphics. So what. Do you think the world is going to beat a path to your door demanding that you sell them all the copies you have and get more? Highly unlikely if most of the world does not even know that your work exists.

Assuming you are like the great majority of unsigned artists, your recording and subsequent release and promotion has two goals: to sell some copies that will help pay the bills and to get you signed to a real record company. Many of the same techniques will help you progress towards both aspirations. The biggest step for most people is learning that it's OK to yell about yourself. Self-promotion can be a difficult area for many people. Somehow, many artists seem to think there is something less than dignified in hustling for anything that you, yourself, created. Are you not proud of your work? Do you not think it worthy of attention? Don't you see big stars in the music industry hustling for their work all the time? If you answer yes to these questions, then you should be able to see how selling your own work is just a part of the process. It is a good thing. In the early stages of your career, you will be your own best agent. If you don't tell folks how good you are, who will?

We in the USA live in a very noisy country, in a very noisy world. We are bombarded by hundreds, if not thousands, of messages every day, all vying for our attention. Thousands of recordings are released every year, and all are aiming to get the same thing: attention. If you expect to have a career in the music business, you need some, too. The key to getting attention is to identify who is most likely to listen and then get your work to them.

Identify sources of free publicity. This includes all local media outlets that might have even a passing interest in you and your activities. A few examples are local commercial radio and television stations, college radio stations, the entertainment sections of local newspapers, even the throwaways, and quite frankly anyone else who has access to more than a few ears. You are not in a position to be too choosy. If a student journalist from the local college newspaper wants a review copy of your recording for a possible piece in their column, I'd get it to them. For all media outlets, communicate with their office and try to get the name of the person who might be most interested in your release. Make it clear who you are and what your activity is and you should be guided to the right person.

Put together a publicity package for your recording before you do anything else. Your publicity package will help convince possible sales outlets and music industry contacts that you are serious about what you do. The package both introduces and recommends you and your work. Unless a member of your band or a friend has writing experience, you might want to consider using a professional or a writing student. Check out the English department of your local college for writing students who might want to help you.

Aside from a copy of your recording, the standard promo kit should include the following.

Bio. Keep your bio to one page. Tell those who have never heard of you what you want them to know. Give them a short history of your band with some description of the type of music you play. Tell them who is in your band and what instruments they play. Have any of the members played with well-known acts? Has the band's music been used in films or included on compilation releases? Have any of the songwriters in the band had their material recorded by other artists? How would you describe your stage act? Has your band played at any hip festivals or opened for any well-known acts? Use some imagination to help make your bio stand out.

Cover letter. A cover letter is a must. Your cover letter should tell the person receiving your press kit stuff why they should be incredibly interested in you and what it is that you want (review my CD, give me a job, mention my band's gig, etc.). State what you want clearly. Don't just expect someone to get the idea. Your cover letter should be no longer than one page. Always mention that you plan to follow up the receipt of your press kit (e.g., "I will call you in a week to confirm receipt of these materials").

One-sheet. This is a brief synopsis of your marketing plan, including condensed info on your touring, radio, retail, and advertising plans. It is used mostly by distributors and retailers who want to see that you are able to market and promote the music they may try and sell.

Photo. An 8x10 black and white is industry standard. Unless you already have what you think is a really great shot of your band, consider hiring a pro. Ask the photog if they know of a vendor who can copy them in bulk. When I say copy, I don't mean Xerox. Even though there are copying machines that can make very good copies of photographs these days, it is considered cheesy to send them with a kit. Get your promo photo copied as a photo. It usually costs no more to have the duplicator add some print, like your name, address, logo, etc. If your photog can't give you the name of a bulk photo copying vendor, check with local modeling services or theatrical agencies. They use promo photos like we use tissues. Put a sticker on the back of each photo you send that identifies the people on the front. If you don't have a phone number and address printed on the front, include this info on the back.

Press clippings. Cut out every mention or article about your act. Photocopy your clippings and staple them together. Always attach the name of the newspaper and the person who wrote the piece. Do not include the date of the clipping as it may make some of your notices look old. Put your most impressive clippings on top. Most people don't read more than the first two or three. Even though most people won't read them all, a nice stack of clippings is a good thing to send because it proves that you are worthy of notice. When you talk to a member of the press, ask what publication they represent and if they can notify you when the piece about you will run. Ask friends to keep on the lookout for mentions of your act in papers outside of your immediate area. Some papers may print something about you without ever talking to you. Newer acts may include everything ever written about them, while more experienced acts have the luxury of picking the best reviews.

Adapt your press kit. Depending on who your press kit is going to, you will want to modify its contents to suit the recipient. Some typical victims might include the following.

Clubs. Always include a list of your previous gigs. Past gigs with other bands can be presented but are secondary. If possible, let the club owner or booking agent know that you are willing and able to promote your gig at their venue and how you intend to do this (via posters, flyers, a mailing list, etc.). Mention what dates you have available. Never talk about money in a press kit. That comes later.

Record labels. Instead of sending your entire CD, consider sending a cassette of two or three of the best songs. Most A&R reps will only listen to this much anyway. Make the cassette copies of the highest quality possible. If you do not feel capable of producing a really high-quality cassette at home, have your studio make a few of the cassettes for you. It is worth the extra cost. If an A&R rep is interested, they will request more songs. This will keep the lines of communication open and active.

Media. The press is always looking for an angle. Some special reason to write about something or someone. Think about what your band is doing that will set you apart. Are you playing a benefit gig? Is yours the first bluegrass band to play in Iceland? Do you all wear pink shoes? Any and all angles will do. Play them up. If you want the press to publicize a particular gig write "Time-sensitive material, use before..." on the outside of the envelope. Always follow up with a phone call.

Some other tips. Put all of your material into a folder with pockets. It is harder for the recipient to lose things this way. Get some artwork, either something printed or a band sticker, on the front of the folder. Be creative and artistic on the outside envelope. You want your package to stand out from a pile of such things on someone's desk.

Look at as many other performers' press kits as you can get your hands on. Go to your local newspaper. They may have old ones that they will let you look at or even have. Everyone is vying for attention just like you. If you get some good ideas from other kits, that's great. Don't copy outright what someone else has said or done; that's not so great. If you have other incredibly cool stuff, like posters, stickers, etc., you might include them also. All of this material should be presented with as much style as you can muster.

Finally, don't forget: A press kit creates an impression before the listener ever presses play. Don't just slap one together. You want your package to be noticed and memorable. Take some time, get creative, and don't cheap out. Your press kit may be the difference between your music getting played or getting canned.

Want to sell some copies of your recording? Of course you do. After your family, friends, and lovers have bought all they can, where do you find new customers? Almost everywhere. The key to good marketing is to target your audience and not waste a lot of time trying to sell your work to people who have very little interest. Go into your local music store. What do you see? Thousands of releases happily waiting to be purchased. How would you begin to make your choice? You would look for the category cards that identify certain sections of music as jazz, blues, rock, new age, and so on. As a customer, you don't think twice about using this information to find your way, but many artists bridle at the thought of labeling their own music.

When attempting to market a musical product, one important thing you will have to do is categorize it. I know, this stinks. Almost everyone thinks that their sound is unique and hates to try and answer the inevitable question: "So, what kind of music do you play?" The problem with not categorizing your music at all is that the entire music industry is categorized. Radio stations, record companies, retailers, almost every level of the business is using categorization to some extent. That's a hell of a trend to try and buck. Even if you feel that your music crosses over several boundaries of categories, you must give people who may be unfamiliar with your sound some kind of clue as to your style. If that means you end up calling your work the world's first country-jazz recording, so be it. At least listeners have some sort of guidepost.

Get your release carried by every music store you can find. Smaller, local music shops are more likely to feature the output of local artists, but don't give up on the megastores either. Chain stores such as Wal-Mart only carry what is purchased by their national buyers, but the managers of music megastores such as Tower Records or Media Play have more leeway to carry local artists. With any size retail outlet, the key to getting stocked is personal contact. Show the store manager that you believe in your product, and let them know what efforts you are making in support of your release (e.g., local gigs, radio airplay, press coverage, etc.). If you can design an imaginative display and get a store to give you some space, this is a good booster for sales. Offer to have special autographed copies available for sale. People love signed copies of anything. Follow up initial stocking in stores by dropping by to find out how sales are going and to make sure that your release is still properly on display. Ask the store manager if there are any other ways that you can help sales of your release. They will be very glad that you show such interest in your product.

Always make sure that you have copies of your release with you at gigs and any other types of personal appearances. Make sure to have a release party. If you have performing engagements around the time of your release, a gig is a good occasion for a release party. Make sure that this fact is featured in advertising for the gig. Offer free copies of your recording, along with tickets to the gig/party, as promotional giveaways to local radio stations. I know many artists who make it a point to never go anywhere without at least a couple copies of their latest release. You never know who you are going to meet.

Get your recording played on the radio. In general, there are two types of radio stations in the US: college and commercial. College stations are numerous and usually much more willing to give airplay to artists who are not affiliated with large recording companies. Almost any college of any size has a student-run radio station. Most of these stations organize their broadcasting time in blocks. This means that they devote certain time periods to specific DJs who play a particular type of music. The best way to get your music played on a college radio station is to get in touch with the station and find out which show or block of time is devoted to your type of music and contact that DJ by name. (For a listing of the associations of college broadcasters, see RESOURCES chapter, "Industry Associations.")

Commercial radio stations will be harder nuts to crack for unsigned artists. Most commercial stations play only one category of music and, even within that category, limit their selection to songs on the charts. This does not mean that they are totally inaccessible to the independent. Commercial radio stations in your area may have a showcase for local talent or they may have a program manager, the person who decides what gets played, who is sympathetic to the plight of unsigned artists. If you are playing at a club that advertises on a commercial station, they may be willing to give your song some play to support your gig and their advertiser. No matter how big and unwelcoming a commercial radio station may seem, it never hurts to try and talk to someone who works there. Even if they don't play your music, they might be able to point you towards someone who will. (For commercial radio stations' industry associations, see RESOURCES chapter, "Industry Associations.")

Obviously I cannot cover all the countless outlets for the promotion of your recording that might be available to you. Fortunately, there are entire books (see RESOURCES chapter) and professional publicity agents that specialize in this field. Get educated. Keep files on all your contacts and possible contacts. When people say, "Get back to me on that," get back to them. If you have a good product and are assertive and confident, without being pushy or overbearing, you will get positive responses. I have found, over the course of the years, that the only things I regret, in terms of promotion, are the things I didn't do. Never neglect to make a call because you think that you don't have a chance. Even if you are rejected by an individual or organization, try not to take it personally. The best and biggest in the business have been refused numerous times. I don't know of anyone who hasn't. A rebuff of your work probably says a lot more about the judgment of the person declining than it does about the quality of your work. There is always someone else to talk to who just may love you and appreciate your musical efforts.

COPYRIGHT PROTECTION AND ROYALTY PAYMENTS

The subjects of copyright protection and royalty payments are full of legal details and subject to changing rules. There are many attorneys who specialize in these areas, simply because of their legal complexity and changing nature. I cannot give you legal advice (I am not a lawyer) or detailed information (there is just too much of it) on either of these subjects. I can give you a general overview on protecting your work and point you in the right direction.

Since February 15, 1972, federal protection for "sound recordings" has been in effect as an amendment to the Copyright Act of 1909. The 1976 Copyright Act made provision for protection of unpublished sound recordings fixed after January 1, 1978. Let's do a little legal stuff.

The Senate Committee on the Judiciary defines a sound recording as follows:

> copyrightable "sound recordings" are original works of authorship comprising an aggregate of musical, spoken, or other sounds that have been fixed in tangible form. The copyrightable work comprises the aggregation of sounds and not the tangible medium of fixation. Thus, "sound recordings" as copyrightable subject matter are distinguished from "phonorecords," the latter being physical objects in which sounds are fixed. They are also distinguished from copyrighted literary, dramatic, or musical works that may be reproduced on a "phonorecord."

Whew! And that's just the start. Feel like calling a lawyer yet? You may not need to, but you can see that copyrights are quite a bit more complex than your average blues chord progression. What can you do for yourself?

I have known some artists who were absolutely paranoid about copyrights, almost to the point of keeping their work under lock and key, afraid to send copies of their recordings to strangers for fear their songs would be stolen. I have also heard many myths about copyright protection floating around over the years. There is no reason for the average musician to waste a lot of energy pitching a wiggy about copyrights.

In terms of copyrights, the most important thing for performers to decide is who is the author of a particular work. The various copyright acts were not designed to fix authorship. There is no formula in the law. It is quite common for the copyrightable elements in a sound recording to involve authorship by both the performers and the producer. Remember, we are talking about the recording of a song, not the song itself. If the recording is prepared either by performers or producer as employees, the employee is the author as the work was done for hire. If there is no agreement with a producer or employment relationship between the artists and another party, the authorship will be owned by the performing artists. If the notice of copyright fails to name the owner, the name of the producer appearing on the recording label or container will be deemed part of the copyright notice. In other words, always put the names of the copyright owners of your recordings right next to the copyright notice on labels and sleeves.

The notice of copyright for a sound recording should contain the following: the letter "P" in a circle, followed by the year of the first public distribution, then the name of the copyright owner. It will look something like this:

℗1996 XYZ Records Corp.

Make sure this type of notice appears on all copies of your recordings that you wish to protect.

You don't have to be a company or corporation to own a copyright to a sound recording. If you are releasing your own recording, individuals and groups can also protect their ownership.

The copyright owner of a sound recording has the exclusive rights to reproduce it, distribute copies to the public, and make derivative works based on the original. This does not mean that you can prevent others from making covers of your music or soundalike recordings that imitate the original. You can't, and they can't stop you from doing the same to their material. If you decide that you want to record a piece of music written by someone other than yourself, it is a real good idea to get permission in writing from them or, if their music is handled by a publishing company, from that company. If you are not known personally by the writer or don't know who represents them, you can contact: Harry Fox Agency, Inc., 711 3rd Avenue, New York, NY, 10017. They are a national agency that represents almost all of the music publishers in the United States and can provide important information if you're recording someone else's song.

Your recording will be deemed published if offered to wholesalers or retailers for ultimate sale to the public. Within three months of the date of publication, the copyright owner must deposit two complete copies of the sound recording to: Copyright Office of the Library of Congress, Washington, D.C. 20559. Publication is defined as the distribution "to the public by sale or other transfer of ownership, or by rental, lease, or lending." You will need to fill out Form SR, which the Copyright Office will send to you on request. This is known as copyright registration. You do not have to register your published or unpublished works to be protected under the law, but no action for infringement of copyright can be brought until registration has been made.

Starting to get confused? I'm not surprised if you are. Some of these requirements, rights, and responsibilities sound contradictory. Copyright law is always changing as new formats are brought to market and new commercial outlets appear every year. The great majority of unsigned artists who are making their first recordings will not have very complicated needs in terms of copyright until they are faced with wide commercial application of their material. By that time you should be seeing a lawyer.

Once you have made a sound recording of your work, you actually have two items to copyright: the song itself and the recording of the song. A piece of music is protected under common law from the moment of inception. In other words, from the moment you think of a song idea, you have certain rights to its protection that can vary from state to state. Even if you record a song and distribute copies, you may not be required to register a copyright with the Copyright Office of the United States in Washington, D.C., to have some protection. If you wish to register the authorship of a song, write to the Copyright Office at the address given above and ask for Form PA. For most unsigned artists, the important thing is not to keep your song a secret until you have a copyright certificate in hand, but to put a notice of copyright on each copy of your material, either written or recorded. Notice of the ownership of a song takes the form of the words: "Copyright, 1996 John Doe." Just substitute the correct year and your name.

For most noncommercial releases, if you clearly show the intent to protect your work and identify the copyright holders, you have some protection under the law. Of course, if you want to register your work with the copyright office, you really can't go wrong there. All you need to do is contact the copyright office, fill out the forms they send you, send back the forms with other required material and a fee, and, bingo, you have your copyright. This does not mean that the government is able to shield you from others who may claim that your song constitutes theft of their song, but it does state your intention to protect your material from unauthorized use by others. The same holds true for copyrighting the recording of your song. Even though you have certain rights without copyright registration, it is always prudent to obtain it as soon as possible.

Everyone who is contemplating signing a contract regarding the release of their recording should find out a lot more about this subject. Your rights and responsibilities change as you enter into commercial publishing and distribution. If you have any questions or doubts about the standing of your work as far as copyrighting is concerned, I strongly suggest that you contact a lawyer specializing in this field or the copyright office in Washington, D.C.

Everyone involved in music should know that when music is used by businesses such as radio stations, movie production companies, and television production companies, as well as when CDs or cassettes are sold to the public, the authors of that music are paid royalties. All the members of a band that score a hit recording may get a percentage of the proceeds from the sale of the recording, but it is the registered authors of the songs alone, unless other agreements have been signed, who get paid when the music is used by other media outlets. These types of royalties are collected and distributed by what are known as performing rights organizations.

The big two in the United States are the American Society of Composers, Authors, and Publishers (ASCAP) and Broadcast Music, Inc. (BMI). These two organizations collect hundreds of millions of dollars a year from broadcasters and others and distribute the money to their registered members. Members can be writers of music and/or lyrics and publishers of this material. These organizations also have grant and awards programs for composers they judge to be of merit. Don't think that you can just become a member and start collecting checks for your music. Not so.

You first need to apply for membership, and then the possibility of distribution payment depends on complex formulas that determine how much your music has actually been broadcast or used in other ways by businesses. These formulas and how they are reported is far too complex a matter for me to go into here. I can say that if you are serious about a career in music and are the author of compositions that are recorded, you would do well to contact both of these organizations and apply for membership in one. You may only be a member of one organization at any given time. When you become a member, you are giving that organization the exclusive right to collect royalties for your music on your behalf. Member dues are very low, and even if you do not qualify for distributions of money, it can only be to your credit to be a member of one of these nationally recognized professional organizations. The day your first recording does hit Number 1, they will know where to send all the loot.

You should assume that all of the above applies to the United States only. If your recordings get into foreign markets, you will have to wrestle with new sets of rules and organizations for each nation, as well as international accords and agreements. Sounds like fun, don't it? Once you get to the point of international distribution, though, if you do not have a lawyer and accountant who are familiar with the business of entertainment, you are stone cold crazy.

Appendix: Spec Deals

The word "spec" stands for speculation. Speculation on the part of one of the signatories to a deal for which they may not get paid. Spec deals can be very attractive and useful, but they can also be very complicated and sometimes quite restrictive.

A very simple example of a spec deal would be for an independent producer to agree to work on your recording project for no money up front. Instead they would get paid when the recording was sold directly to the public, to a music company, or both. On quick inspection, you might think this sounds wonderful. You could get all types of services on spec and not have to pay until your masterpiece is rocketing up the charts. Great! In theory, yes; in reality, not always so great.

One drawback to spec deals is that the party doing work on spec will usually be asking for a larger payment than if you had cash up front. What might have been $1000 of studio time for cash could end up costing quite a bit more on spec. The logic behind this is that the studio is waiting to be paid and is taking the very real risk that they may never get paid. You may never sell the recording. Some spec deals specify payment in the form of a percentage of artist royalties. In these cases, the artist could find themselves paying for years. If you were to sign spec deals with a studio, a producer, an engineer, a duplicating house, a distributor, and a publicist, you might find yourself in the position of signing away all your royalties. Why would anyone sign a deal like this? Because they have absolutely no other way to pay for services, and they will never have a career if they don't get into a studio.

Another problem with being on spec is that the person or business you have made the deal with is likely to give preference to their cash customers. This puts you in second or third place for the attention you were counting on when you made the deal. It can get very frustrating to have your appointments broken and sessions postponed because your spec deal partner is off making money.

There are other ways spec deals can bite you in the butt. In this little tale, the wide-eyed band attracts the attention of a large, multimillion dollar studio in New York City. One of the two partners who owns said spaceship of a studio likes the band and is willing to record them on spec. The other partner is not enthusiastic but says OK. The band makes a deal with the partner who thinks they are swell, and the band believes it will offer them enough time to record an album's worth of material. No paper is signed. A handshake gets the band on its way. Since the studio has 32-track digital capability, the highest tech in the world at that point, they decide to use that format rather than the more widely used 24-track analog, which the studio also possesses. Might as well use the best they have as long as it's there.

Assuming that the deal is solid, the band records rhythm and backing tracks for ten songs, then something goes wrong. One of the studio's partners sells his share to the other, and now there is only one owner. Guess which one. That's right, the partner who was not that interested in the deal in the first place is now the sole owner of the studio and calls a halt to the band's recording. Nothing will revive the deal, and the band thinks of finishing the album at its own expense at another studio. Unfortunately, the recording format they have used is only found in other world-class studios charging upward of $300 an hour for the privilege of using their facilities. To make a long story short, the unfinished master tapes still reside in my basement. Spec deal gone awry.

What could this band have done differently to protect themselves? First off, they should have gotten the deal in writing. This was a fairly big project and should have had at least a letter of agreement signed by all parties. Spec deals and their agreements can be simple or complicated. Even the simple ones should at least have a letter drawn up that states what each party expects to get out of the deal and what they are required to put in. All involved should sign this letter and have a copy. The larger and more complicated your deal becomes, the more you may need an actual contract with a lawyer. If anyone offers you a contract for a spec deal, I would strongly advise having a lawyer look at it before you sign.

The second thing the band could have done is to have chosen the less high-tech but more common 24-track analog recording format. If they had used the more popular machine, they would have had a much better chance of finding a studio they could afford in which to finish their work. With the rarified, high-tech, expensive format, they were backed into the economic position of not being able to complete the tape.

Our singers and strummers could also have planned their sessions differently. If they had taken one or two songs at a time to completion, even when the deal fell apart they would have had something finished. With even two finished songs, they might have been able to convince someone else to help them do more. With ten unfinished songs, they were pretty much dead in the water.

Don't let the preceding examples and warnings put you totally off any kind of spec deal. Many famous artists got their starts this way, and a good spec deal might be the beginning of great things for you. If someone offers to work with you, or you are trying to get someone to give you their services on spec, consider the entire situation in detail. The watchwords here are be careful. Don't rush into things. Don't back yourself into a corner. And have a backup plan if your deal falls apart.

Postscript

If you have just finished reading this book cover to cover, you may be starting to feel overwhelmed with details. Don't worry. Take a deep breath and relax. I have included many different scenarios in this book to try and address all types of recording situations. Your sessions will probably be far less complicated. Even if you are embarking on a complex, detail-filled project, it is possible to keep everything under control and stay sane.

All of the advice in this book is designed to help you do just that. If you can keep the details of your projects organized, and thereby stay sane, it is much more probable that your sessions will be productive and big fun. It's when everyone is relaxed and having fun in a recording studio that the really good stuff happens.

I am very interested in hearing how your sessions go and any comments readers might have concerning this book. I can be reached at P.O. Box 640163, Oakland Gardens, NY 11364-0163; e-mail: jayce@javanet.com.

Thanks for reading and good luck!

Glossary

The following are some terms you may come across in your recording studio adventures. This is not a complete listing of all musical and technical terms used in studios but is a list of the most likely everyday terms used by musicians and studio personnel.

amplifier: A device that increases the voltage, current, or power of an incoming signal as a proportion of the incoming amplitude, by adding power from another source. Usually connected to loudspeakers, it makes small sounds louder. The power of an amplifier is directly proportional to the number of times the operator will hear the expression, "Turn that thing down!" Called an "amp" for short.

amplitude: The magnitude of a signal, measured by determining the amount of fluctuation in air pressure (of a sound) or voltage (of an electrical signal). When the signal is in the audio range, the amplitude is perceived as loudness.

analog: An electronic device capable of exhibiting continuous electrical fluctuations that correspond in a one-to-one ratio with the audio output. Any musical device that does not use digital technology to create, process, or store its signal is known as analog. Some equipment uses a combination of digital and analog technologies.

capsule: The section of a microphone that picks up sound and converts it to an electrical impulse.

cardioid microphone: A directional microphone that is most sensitive to sounds coming from the front of the mic and rejects sounds coming from the rear of the mic.

CD-R: Acronym for compact disc-recordable. A digital recording format using recordable audio compact discs. The recorded discs are compatible with any CD player.

channel: The electronics of a recording console are organized into channels. Each channel of a recording console will be able to adjust the parameters of a given signal independent of the other channels. Professional recording consoles may have one hundred or more channels. Recording consoles have channels, tape and disk recorders have tracks.

click track: An electronic metronome that produces a steady click or audible pulse that may be recorded to help keep musicians at a specific tempo.

compressor: An electronic device that controls the dynamic range of a signal. The effect that a compressor creates is called compression.

cut: (1) noun: A piece of music, speech, or sound, separate and distinct from other sections on a common reproduction medium. (2) verb: To reduce the amplitude of a given signal.

DAT: Acronym for digital audio tape. A digital tape recording format.

delay: An electronic device that will repeat a signal. Sometimes called an echo device.

demo: Short for demonstration recording. Indicates that the artist, producer, or record company does not consider the recording to be finished or of sufficient quality for commercial release.

digital: Music and recording equipment that uses computer technology to convert an electronic signal into a stream of numbers that can be processed or stored as numbers and then reconverted into an electronic signal. The advantages of this method of signal processing and storage include less noise and truer fidelity. There is much argument as to which is better, analog or digital.

direct box: A device that converts the signal from an electric or electronic instrument or amplifier to one which a recording console can accept at its input. Called a "DI" for short.

dry: A sound recorded with no added effects.

dynamic range: The difference between the softest and loudest sound in a musical piece or the signals captured, reproduced, or generated by an audio recorder or device.

effects: Term which loosely covers audio processing devices such as reverbs and delays that enhance the dry signal. Short for special effects.

engineer: A person educated and trained in the operation, massaging, and tweaking of audio equipment.

equalizer: An electronic device that shapes the tonal profile or frequency content of an audio signal. Simple types are the tone controls on a stereo or guitar amplifier. More sophisticated units give fine control over specific frequencies. Often expressed as "EQ."

fader: A linear device found on recording consoles that controls amplitude.

feedback: A cycle in which the output of a device is fed back into its own input. When this happens with microphones, amplifiers, and speakers, a fearful earful occurs.

filter: A device for eliminating selected frequencies from the sound spectrum of an incoming signal.

flanging: A time delay effect that gives a swooshing character to an audio signal.

frequency: The number of times a periodic waveform cycles, or repeats, over a given period of time. Expressed in hertz. Low frequencies are bass tones; high frequencies are treble tones.

gain: The ratio of boost or attenuation of a signal between input and output.

graphic equalizer: A type of equalizer that has multiple sliding controls corresponding to each band of frequencies that will give a visual representation of the frequency spectrum curve created by moving the sliders.

head: The beginning of a song, a recording, or a reel of tape.

high-speed dubbing: A means of copying one tape to another in which both machines are synchronized to operate at higher than normal speed. Generally considered to be inferior in tonal quality and signal-to-noise ratio than real-time copying.

hit: A very popular recording. (See **money**.)

input: The point at which a signal enters an electronic circuit.

J-card: The card inserted into a cassette box on which the information for the enclosed cassette is printed. The card resembles a "J" when viewed from its end.

jack: A device connected to electrical equipment or an electrical cable that will accept a plug of corresponding design to make temporary electrical connections.

lay down: (1) To record. "The band will lay down tracks starting at 2:00." (2) What you will want to do after a 16-hour session.

limiter: An electronic device that restricts the dynamic range of a signal. When you use an audio limiter, you are said to "limit" the signal.

line level: A signal level typically -10dBV for home and semipro audio equipment and +4dBm for professional equipment.

master: (1) noun: The final version of a recording judged by all involved to be worthy of release. You may hear a recording described as being of master, meaning high, quality. (2) verb: The act and process of converting a recording from a professional to a consumer format.

mic: Short for microphone. "Mike" is a name.

MIDI: Acronym for musical instrument digital interface. Developed in the early 1980s by a consortium of music synthesizer manufacturers: Yamaha, Roland, Korg, Kawai, and Sequential Circuits. MIDI is a method of communicating music performance data among musical instruments and other types of electronic equipment.

minidisc: A digital format, developed by Sony, that allows up to 74 minutes of digital audio to fit onto a 64mm recordable, erasable magneto-optical disk.

mix: (1) noun: A version of a piece of music that has had its tracks adjusted for tone, position, volume, etc. and has been transferred to a master recorder, usually a 2-track stereo version. The resulting master recording is known as a mix. (2) verb: The act of adjusting the tone, position, volume, etc. of the various tracks of a recorded piece of music.

mix session: A period of time in a recording studio devoted solely to the process of mixing.

mixer: An electronic device very much like a recording console but built to be used mainly for live sound reinforcement. (See **recording console**.)

monaural: Having one audio channel.

money: One of the perks of having a hit. (See **hit**.)

monitor: (1) noun: The speakers in a recording studio control room used to listen to the recording console's output. A speaker designed to be used as a recording studio monitor is much more accurate and built to very different specifications than a home stereo speaker. (2) verb: To listen to the output of an audio device.

multitrack: Any recording device that has more than two discrete tracks for storage of audio information.

mute: To silence the output of a recording console channel or other device. Recording consoles may have mute buttons that allow the engineer to silence a channel's output without disturbing the fader.

outboard equipment: Electronic equipment that is not physically contained in the recording console or recording machines. This term is used collectively to describe devices such as reverb units, delay devices, compressors, limiters, etc.

output: The point at which a signal leaves an electronic circuit.

overdub: (1) verb: The process of adding material to a previously recorded section. (2) noun: The sections of material added to a previously recorded section.

pan pot: Short for panorama potentiometer. The rotary device or "knob" on a recording console that controls the left-right position of a channel's output in the stereo soundfield. Rotate the pan pot full counterclockwise and that channel's signal will be heard in the left monitor speaker only. The left-right balance control on your stereo is a kind of pan pot. (See **pot**.)

patch: To connect together, as with the inputs and outputs of audio devices, often with patch cords.

patch bay: A device to which the inputs and outputs of many separate devices are connected and therefore brought together so as to be convenient for changing connections.

phase shifter: A time delay signal processor that creates a swirling effect known as "phasing."

plug: A device attached to an electrical cable used to make temporary connections to electrical equipment.

pot: Short for potentiometer. A type of variable resistor most often used as a rotary volume or tone control. The volume knob on a guitar is a pot.

punch-in: The replacing of a section of music already recorded with a new version of the section on its original track. For instance, if a bass player has played a good version of a song but has made a mistake in one section, that section can be replaced by having the bass player play the appropriate section, at the correct place in the piece, and having the engineer punch-in or press the record button at the right time. The old version will be erased and the new version recorded. On tape-based recording systems, punch-ins destroy the original track in the section being punched in. On disk-based digital systems, it is possible to perform nondestructive punch-ins.

punch-out: The point at which a punch-in is supposed to end is called the punch-out. You might hear the process described in this way: "Punch-in the guitar track at 2:35:09 and punch-out at 2:42:55." The numbers refer to the time code that professional tape recorders generate to keep track of where you are on a song.

rackmount: Equipment designed to fit into industry standard 19-inch wide racks and cases.

R-DAT: A way of referring to a DAT cassette or machine.

real time: A means of recording or manipulating audio or data as it occurs. Making a copy of a phonograph record to tape must be performed in real time. One way of making tape copies is in real time as opposed to high-speed dubbing.

recording console: An electronic device that controls the various signals generated by sound sources, instruments, voices, recording machines, and processing devices in a recording studio. A recording console can be small enough to fit on your lap or over ten feet long.

release: (1) verb: To put a recording on sale to the public or distribute it widely. (2) noun: The last stage of the waveform that a sound creates. The point at which a sound falls to an inaudible or unreadable level.

reverb: Short for reverberation. (1) noun: The decaying signal that results from a sound bouncing off the environment in which it was produced. (2) noun: An electronic device or effect that gives the impression of a sound having occurred in a room or a hall.

roll-off: To attenuate or reduce a signal.

sample: (1) noun: A small section of another recording, a short sound, or musical phrase usually stored on a digital storage and retrieval system. (2) verb: To record a short piece of material on a sampler.

sampler: An electronic device that can store short pieces of material for retrieval or triggering by other devices such as sequencers or keyboard instruments.

sequencer: A computer that can store and generate information that will direct the action of other devices such as synthesizers, effects devices, recorders, etc. A powerful sequencer can direct an entire recording with no humans playing the instruments. We humans still have to program them, though. Heh, heh.

signal: When a sound has been converted into an electronic pulse, that pulse is described as a signal.

signal-to-noise ratio: The ratio between the level of a signal at a reference point in a circuit and the level of electrical noise at the same point in a circuit. Expressed as "dB" and many times written as "S/N." The higher the S/N number, the less noise present.

slate: A slate is a recorded announcement at the beginning of a take that identifies what follows. This announcement should always include the title of the piece and the take number. A slate may also include the artist, date, producer, or any other information deemed necessary to properly identify the recording. A slate may be performed by the engineer, producer, or artist. A slate should always precede each new take.

SMPTE: Acronym for the Society of Motion Picture and Television Engineers. SMPTE time code is a synchronization standard adopted in the United States in the early 1960s for video tape editing. Although developed for video and still the standard for video editing, SMPTE has been accepted by the audio industry and is widely used for audio synchronizing tasks.

solo: A feature on a recording console that allows the recording engineer to push a button and cut off all channels being heard except for the channel(s) being soloed. This feature allows an engineer to listen to each channel individually without using the faders to mute the other channels.

sound board: (See **recording console**.)

sound desk: (See **recording console**.)

spec: Short for speculation. A product or service delivered with the promise of payment at a later date is referred to as being "on spec."

specs: Short for specifications. The information reflecting the electronic performance and electrical requirements of a device.

super cardioid microphone: A variant of the cardioid that rejects sounds from the rear of the mic. A super cardioid mic is designed to have a more narrow, or super tight, pick-up pattern than a regular cardioid mic. Super in this case doesn't necessarily mean better, just different.

tail: The end of a section of a recording or a reel of tape.

take: A complete or incomplete recorded version of a whole or partial piece of music. Music that is played in a studio but not recorded is never a take. If, during a session, you have been rehearsing a piece of music and the engineer asks if you are ready to go for a take, they are asking if you are ready to try and record what you have been rehearsing. Different recorded versions of a particular piece of music will be slated and labeled "Take 1," "Take 2," and so on.

talkback: The talkback system is a microphone in the studio control room that is connected to allow people in the control room to communicate with people in the recording room. This may be through the artist's headphones or through speakers. The talkback microphone can also be used by the engineer to slate takes.

timbre: The tonal profile of a sound. Many times expressed as "tone." The timbre is made up of a sound's harmonic profile. Timbre is the main way that the human ear distinguishes one sound from another.

time code: A system of electronic pulses which can be recorded and is used to synchronize the operation of two or more audio or video devices.

top: The beginning of a section of a recording.

topping and tailing: The process of cleaning up all unwanted sounds at the beginning and end of a section of a recording.

track: A discrete channel of information that a given machine can store and/or generate on tape or disk. Information on a track can be recorded and played back independently of all other tracks. A stereo cassette recorder has two tracks: left and right. We could just as easily call them one and two. A professional multitrack recorder can have sixty-four or more tracks. Tape and disk recorders and sequencers have tracks, recording consoles have channels.

TRS: Acronym for tip, ring, sleeve. Denotes a phone or TT (tiny telephone) plug that has three connector sections. Commonly used on headphone plugs and balanced audio patch cords.

trigger: (1) noun: A device that creates an electronic signal to control the activity of a separate piece of electronic equipment. (2) verb: To cause a piece of electronic equipment to respond to an outside signal. A sampler can be triggered by a sequencer.

tweak: To fine tune or adjust.

tweeter: A loudspeaker designed to reproduce high frequencies.

valve: In England, a vacuum tube like those used in guitar amplifiers.

volt: The International System unit of electrical potential and electromotive force, equal to the difference of electrical potential between two points on a conducting wire carrying a constant current of one ampere when the power dissipated between the points is one watt.

volume: Common term, technically incorrect, used to indicate the loudness of an amplified sound.

watt: A unit of power in the International System equal to one joule (unit of measurement) per second. Watts can be calculated in three ways: as the product of the voltage and the current (VI), the voltage squared divided by the resistance (V^2/R), or the current squared times the resistance (I^2R). Named for James Watt, inventor of the steam engine and a real smart guy.

wet: A sound that has had effects added to it.

woofer: A speaker designed to reproduce low frequencies.

workstation: Any computer, usually disk-based equipment, that can store, edit, and manipulate recorded information. Musicians may use keyboard workstations to store and manipulate musical information. Recording studios use audio workstations.

XLR: A type of locking, multipin cable connector frequently used in professional audio equipment. Can have three, four, or five connection pins. Seen mainly on microphones and console inputs. Developed by ITT/Cannon. Sometimes called a Cannon plug.

X-Y miking: A technique for using two microphones, typically cardioid, whereby the two mics cross at an angle of 90 to 130 degrees, capsules close together, to produce a well-balanced stereo image.

Resources

BOOKS FOR FURTHER READING

Mix Bookshelf: c/o Whitehurst & Clark, Inc., 100 Newfield Ave., Edison, NJ 08837-3817, U.S. and Canada: (800) 233-9604, International: (908) 417-9575. This company distributes many valuable how-to and help books, videos, and audio tapes having to do with the music business and recording/musical equipment. Most of the books listed here are available through them. I strongly suggest you send for their free mail order catalog.

This Business of Music, 7th Ed. by Sidney Shemel and M. William Krasilovsky
The nuts and bolts on doing business in the music industry. Detailed explanations of the legal, practical, and procedural problems encountered by everyone in the music business. An essential for professionals.

Getting Radio Airplay, 2nd Ed. by Gary Hustwit
Advice on getting your release on the air. College and commercial radio directories.

Modern Recording Techniques, 4th Ed. by Huber & Runstein
Considered one of the bibles of professional recording. Supplies many clear explanations of the gear you will find in today's recording studios.

Music Producers: Conversations with Today's Top Record Makers by the Editors of *Mix*

The Musician's Business & Legal Guide by Mark Halloran, Ed.
Accessible book on music business and law.

The Musician's Home Recording Handbook by Ted Greenwald
Emphasizes techniques for getting the best sound out of your available equipment.

Recording Industry Sourcebook from Cardinal Business Media
Exhaustive national listings of companies and professionals including record labels and distributors, management, attorneys, agencies, publishing, promotion, marketing, publicity, media, recording studios, mastering, producers, engineers, equipment rental and sales, CD and cassette duplication and manufacturing, music video, photographers, designers, and more.

Releasing an Independent Record, 5th Ed. by Gary Hustwit
How to run your own record label and market your music on a national level.

Sound Advice: The Musician's Guide to the Recording Studio by Wayne Wadhams
Practical, nontechnical tips on topics that will help you sound good.

PERFORMING RIGHTS SOCIETIES
These organizations collect and distribute royalties on behalf of their members.

American Society of Composers, Authors & Publishers (ASCAP)
One Lincoln Plaza, New York, NY 10023; (212) 621-6000
2 Music Square West, Nashville, TN 37203; (615) 742-5000
7920 Sunset Blvd., Ste. 300, Los Angeles, CA 90046; (213) 883-1000
1608 W. Belmont Ave., Ste. 200, Chicago, IL 60657; (312) 472-1157
52 Haymarket, Suites 10 & 11, London, SW1 Y4RP, England; (71) 973-0069
Office 505, 1519 Ponce de Leon Ave., Santurce, Puerto Rico 00910; (809) 725-1688

Broadcast Music, Inc. (BMI)
320 West 57th St., New York, NY 10019; (212) 586-2000
8730 Sunset Blvd. 3rd Floor, Los Angeles, CA 90069; (213) 659-9109
10 Music Square East, Nashville, TN 37203; (615) 291-6700
79 Harley House, Marylebone Rd., London; (71) 935-8517

Canadian Musical Reproduction Rights Agency (CMRRA)
56 Wellesley St. West, Ste. 320, Toronto, Ont. M5S 2S3 Canada; (416) 926-1966

SESAC
55 Music Square East, Nashville, TN 37203; (615) 320-0055
156 West 56th Street, New York, NY 10019; (212) 586-3450

SOCAN
41 Valleybrook Dr., Don Mills, ON, M3B 2S6, Canada; (416) 445-8700
1201 W. Pender St., Ste. 400, Vancouver, BC, V6E 2V2; (604) 669-5569

INDUSTRY ASSOCIATIONS
I did not think it necessary to include descriptions of the focus of the follow-ing groups, as they are self explanatory. These associations are some of the ones that I felt might interest those involved with recording. There are many more industry associations covering every field in recording and music. Many are too localized or too specialized to be included in this book. If you wish a more exhaustive listing, see entries in "Further Reading." Get in touch with all the associations that pertain to your area of interest. You may not want to join them all, but they might have programs or information that will interest you.

Academy of Country Music
6255 Sunset Blvd., Ste. 923, Hollywood, CA 90028; (213) 462-2351

Affiliated Independent Record Companies (AIRCO)
PO Box 241648, Los Angeles, CA 90024; (213) 208-2104

American Composers Alliance
170 West 74th Street, New York, NY 10023; (212) 362-8900

American Federation of Musicians (The Union)
1501 Broadway, Ste. 600, New York, NY 10036; (212) 869-1330
There are branches of the union, or "locals," all over the United States. Many
of the locals offer services to members including musicians referrals, help in
finding music copyists and arrangers, health insurance, discount recording
facilities, etc. Look up your local and find out what they can help you with.

American Guild of Musical Artists (AGMA)
230 West 55th St., New York, NY 10019; (212) 265-3687

American MIDI Users Group
4306 Pineridge Dr., Garland, TX 75042; (214) 272-0963

American Women Composers Inc.
1690 36th St. NW, Suite 409, Washington, DC 20007; (202) 342-8179

Association of Professional Recording Services Ltd. (APRS)
2 Windsor Sq., Reading, Berkshire, RG1 2TH, UK RG1 2TH; (173) 475-6218

Audio Engineering Society
60 East 42nd St., New York, NY 10165; (212) 661-8528
2603 Elm Hill Pike, Nashville, TN 37214; (615) 259-3625

B.C. Country Music Association
4th Fl., 177 West 7th Ave., Vancouver, B.C. V5Y 1L8; (604) 876-4110

Bay Area Music Alliance
22470 Foothill Blvd., Ste. 34, Hayward, CA 94541; (415) 538-0799
(Non-profit career assistance organization)

Canadian Independent Record Production Association
202-144 Front St. W., Toronto, ON, M5J 2L7, Canada; (416) 593-1665

College Music Society
1444 15th St., Boulder, CO 80302; (303) 449-1611

Country Music Association
1 Music Cir. S., Nashville, TN 37203; (615) 244-2840

Entertainment Industry Referral & Assistance Center
1918 Magnolia Blvd., Burbank, CA 91506; (818) 848-9997
(Consultation/substance abuse & mental health)

Hearing Education & Awareness for Rockers (H.E.A.R.)
PO Box 460847, San Francisco, CA 94146-0847; (415) 441-9081

Home Recording Rights Coalition
1145 19th St. NW, Box 33576, Washington, DC 20033; (800) 282-TAPE

Independent Music Producers Syndicate (IMPS)
70 Rte. 202 N., Peterborough, NH 03458; (800) 677-8838

Intercollegiate Broadcasting System
Box 592, Vails Gate, NY 12584; (914) 565-6710

International Bluegrass Association (IBMA)
207 E. 2nd St., Owenboro, KY 42303; (502) 684-9025

International Entertainment Buyers Association
PO Box 100513, Nashville, TN 37224; (615) 259-2400

International League of Women Composers
South Shore Rd., Box 670, Three Mile Bay, NY 13693; (315) 649-5086

International MIDI Association
5316 West 57th St., Los Angeles, CA 90056; (213) 649-MIDI

International Tape/Disc Association
505 8th Ave., New York, NY 10018; (212) 643-0620

Library of Congress, Copyright Office
Washington, DC 20559; (202) 707-3000

Los Angeles Music Network
PO Box 8934, Universal City, CA 91608-8934; (818) 769-6095

Musicians Against AIDS
2336 Market St., Ste. 22, San Francisco, CA 94102; (415) 252-7605

National Academy of Popular Music
875 3rd Ave., 8th Floor, New York 10022; (212) 319-1444

National Academy of Recording Arts & Sciences
157 W. 57th St. #902, New York, NY 10019; (212) 245-5440
410 S. Michigan Ave. #921, Chicago, IL 60605; (312) 786-1121
1227 Spring St. NW, Atlanta, GA 30309; (414) 875-1440
944 Market St. #510, San Francisco, CA 94102; (415) 433-7112
2 Music Cir. S., Nashville, TN 37203; (615) 255-8777
4444 Riverside Dr. #201, Burbank, CA 91505; (818) 843-8253
315 Beale St., Memphis, TN 38103; (901) 525-5500

National Association of Broadcasters (NAB)
1771 N. St. NW, Washington, DC 20036-2891; (202) 429-5300

National Association of College Broadcasters (NACB)
71 George St., Box 1824, Providence RI 02912; (401) 863-2225

National Association of Composers
Barrington Station, Box 49652, Los Angeles, CA 90049; (213) 541-8213
(Association for composers of classical music)

National Association of Independent Record Distributors & Manufacturers
(NAIRD)
1000 Maplewood Dr., Ste. 211, Maple Shade, NJ 08052; (609) 482-8999

National Association of Recording Merchandisers
11 Eves Dr., Ste. 140, Marlton, NJ 08053; (609) 596-2221

National Jazz Service Organization
PO Box 50152, Washington, DC 20004-0152; (202) 347-2604

National Music Publishers Association
205 East 42nd St., 18th Fl., New York, NY 10017; (212) 370-5330

New Music Seminar
632 Broadway, 9th Fl., New York, NY 10012; (212) 473-4343

Northwest Area Music Association
611 E. Howell, Seattle, WA 98122; (206) 322-9247

Pacific Music Industry Association
302-68 Water Street, Vancouver, BC V6B 1A4, Canada; (604) 684-8841

Radio Network Association
1440 Broadway, 5th Fl., New York, NY 10018; (212) 382-2273

Recording Musicians Association
817 Vine St., Ste. 209, Hollywood, CA 90038; (213) 462-4RMA

Society of Professional Audio Recording Services (SPARS)
4300 10th Avenue N., Ste. 2, Lake Worth, FL 33461; (417) 641-6648

Songwriters Guild of America
6430 Sunset Blvd., Hollywood, CA 90028; (213) 462-1108
276 Fifth Ave., Ste. 306, New York, NY 10001; (212) 686-6820
1222 16th Ave. S., Ste. 25, Nashville, TN 37212-2926; (615) 329-1782

Women in Music National Network
31121 Mission Blvd., Ste. 123, Hayward, CA 94544; (510) 471-1752

Women's Independent Label Distribution (WILD)
5505 Delta Road, Lansing, MI 48906; (517) 323-4325

Index

A Music Bookstore At Your Fingertips...

FREE!

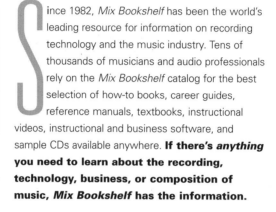

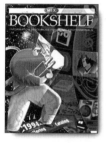

Since 1982, *Mix Bookshelf* has been the world's leading resource for information on recording technology and the music industry. Tens of thousands of musicians and audio professionals rely on the *Mix Bookshelf* catalog for the best selection of how-to books, career guides, reference manuals, textbooks, instructional videos, instructional and business software, and sample CDs available anywhere. **If there's *anything* you need to learn about the recording, technology, business, or composition of music, *Mix Bookshelf* has the information.**

We offer:

• The most comprehensive listing of resources for music industry professionals and hobbyists

• Convenient and cost-efficient "one-stop shopping" for retailers and school bookstores

• Discount and review copies for educators and established music business and recording programs

For a free *Mix Bookshelf* catalog call (800) 233-9604

or write to
Mix Bookshelf; c/o Whitehurst & Clark, Inc.;
100 Newfield Ave.; Edison, NJ 08837-3817
(908) 417-9575; Fax (908) 225-1562

or check us out on the Web! You can browse our catalog and order Bookshelf items at **http://www.mixbookshelf.com**

You'll find information on hundreds of topics including:

Career Development
Studio Business
Music Business Software
Resource Guides
Music Publishing
The Internet
Music Business
Studio Recording
Engineering
Studio Design and Construction
Home Recording
Live Sound
Lighting
Handbooks
Dictionaries
Construction Projects
Maintenance
Digital Audio
Audio for Video and Film
MIDI Guides
MIDI Software Manuals
Multimedia
Synthesis
Computer Music
Instrument-Specific Guides
Samples
Sound Effects
CD-ROMs
Music Theory
Songwriting
Arranging
Lyrics
Composing Alternatives
Instructional Software
Performance
Vocal Training
Keyboards
Guitar
Bass
Rhythm Section
Drums
Saxophone
Accessories